# Target 3
## Get back on track

# AQA GCSE (9–1)
# English Language
# Reading

## David Grant

Pearson

# Contents

# ① Tackling an unseen text

This unit will help you tackle an unseen text. The skills you will build are to:

- identify key ideas in the text
- track how the writer's ideas develop in the text
- explore how the writer's ideas help to achieve their purpose and intention
- check your understanding of the text.

In the exam, you will face questions like the one below. This is about the source on page 2. This unit will prepare you to write your own response to this question.

**Exam-style question**

Read again the first part of the source, from **lines 1 to 7**.

List **four** things from this part of the source about the village of Midwich. (4 marks)

The three key questions in the **skills boosts** will help you tackle an unseen text.

**1** How do I identify the key ideas in the text?

**2** How do I track the writer's purpose and intention?

**3** How do I know I have understood the text?

Read the extract on page 2 from *The Midwich Cuckoos* by John Wyndham, published in 1957. You will tackle a 20th- or 21st-century fiction extract in the Reading section of your Paper 1 exam.

## As you read, remember the following:

**Before reading the extract,** carefully read any introduction provided. It is intended to help you understand where the text is taken from and other useful background information you might need.

**While reading the extract,** if you lose understanding of the text, stop and re-read from the last sentence or paragraph that you clearly understood.

**After reading the extract,** read it again.

Richard and his wife, Janet, were on their way home to the peaceful village of Midwich after an overnight stay in London. They found soldiers blocking the road and refusing to let them pass. The couple have decided they will have to walk home across fields.

**Source A** The Midwich Cuckoos, John Wyndham

We locked the car, climbed the gate, and started over the field of stubble keeping well in to the hedge. At the end of that we came to another field of stubble and bore leftwards across it, slightly uphill. It was a big field with a good hedge on the far side, and we had to go further left to find a gate we could climb. Half-way across the pasture beyond brought us to the top of the rise, and we were able to look out across Midwich — not that much

5 of it was visible for trees, but we could see a couple of wisps of greyish smoke lazily rising, and the church spire sticking up by the elms. Also, in the middle of the next field I could see four or five cows lying down, apparently asleep.

I am not a countryman, I only live there, but I remember thinking rather far back in my mind that there was something not quite right about that. Cows folded up, chewing cud, yes, commonly enough; but cows lying down

10 fast asleep, well, no. But it did not do more at the time than give me a vague feeling of something out of true. We went on.

We climbed the fence of the field where the cows were and started across that, too.

A voice **hallooed** at us, away on the left. I looked round and made out a khaki-clad figure in the middle of the next field. He was calling something unintelligible, but the way he was waving his stick was without doubt a sign for us

15 to go back. I stopped.

'Oh, come on, Richard. He's miles away,' said Janet impatiently, and began to run on ahead.

I still hesitated, looking at the figure who was now waving his stick more energetically than ever, and shouting more loudly, though no more intelligibly. I decided to follow Janet. She had perhaps twenty yards start of me by now, and then, just as I started off, she staggered, collapsed without a sound, and lay quite still.

20 I stopped dead. That was involuntary. If she had gone down with a twisted ankle, or had simply tripped I should have run on, to her. But this was so sudden and so complete that for a moment I thought, idiotically, that she had been shot.

The stop was only momentary. Then I went on again. Dimly I was aware of the man away on the left still shouting, but I did not bother about him. I hurried towards her . . .

25 But I did not reach her.

I went out so completely that I never even saw the ground come up to hit me . . .

hallooed: shouted

# 1 How do I identify the key ideas in the text?

When you first read an unseen text, you need to identify the key ideas and information in each section of the text.

① Read the first paragraph of the extract on page 2.

Look at some ideas and information that the writer has included.

A | Richard and Janet lock their car.

B | They cross two fields so it's quite a long way to walk.

C | After a while, they can see the village of Midwich.

D | They hear the church bells ringing.

E | Everything in Midwich looks perfectly normal.

Label (✎) each piece of information above to identify whether you think it is:

- the key idea of the first paragraph, write (✎) **KEY**
- additional detail, write (✎) **DETAIL**
- not included in the first paragraph, mark with a (✕).

② Now look at the rest of the extract.

a Write (✎) **one** sentence summarising the main idea in each section.

Paragraphs 2 and 3 (lines 8–12): ............................................................................

............................................................................................................................

Paragraph 4 (lines 13–15): ....................................................................................

............................................................................................................................

Paragraphs 5–7 (lines 16–22): ...............................................................................

............................................................................................................................

Paragraphs 8–10 (lines 23–26): .............................................................................

............................................................................................................................

b Now check your answers to question ② a to make sure you have:

- focused on the main idea in each section
- not focused on additional details which are less important than the main idea.

Tick (✓) any that you are happy with and change (✎) any that you are not happy with.

## 2 How do I track the writer's purpose and intention?

Every text has:
- **a purpose**: the reason it was written, for example, to give information or to explain how to do something
- **an intention**: the impact that the writer intends the text to have on the reader, for example, to interest the reader or to change their opinion.

Identifying and tracking the **purpose** and **intention** of an unseen text is a very effective way to develop your understanding of it.

① **a** Which of these **purposes** does the extract on page 2 have? Tick ✓ at least **one**.

argue
☐ | to express the writer's opinion on a topic and influence the reader's opinion

narrate
☐ | to tell a story

inform
☐ | to give the reader information

explain
☐ | to tell the reader how to do something or how something happened

describe
☐ | to create a clear impression of a person, event or situation

**b** Find **one** section or sentence in the text where the writer has achieved **each** purpose you have ticked. Underline Ⓐ and label ✏ it/them.

② Now think about the writer's intention in the extract on page 2.

**a** What impressions, thoughts or feelings does the writer want the reader to have when they read this extract? Tick ✓ any of the impressions below that you were given by the extract.

A.
i. Something strange and disturbing is happening. What's going on? ☐

B.
ii. This is a dangerous situation. ☐

C.
iii. This is a tense situation. How will it end? ☐

**b** Find **one** section or sentence in the text where the writer created **each** impression you have ticked. Circle Ⓐ and label ✏ it/them.

**c** What do you think is happening in Midwich? Write ✏ **one** sentence summing up your impressions of the situation described in the extract **and** how the writer has created them.

.......................................................................................................................

.......................................................................................................................

.......................................................................................................................

.......................................................................................................................

**3** **How do I know I have understood the text?**

One way to check your understanding of a text is to try to sum up its main ideas and the impression it creates in just one sentence.

**1** Look at some students' summaries of the text on page 2.

**a** Which one most accurately sums up the main ideas in the text? Tick ✓ it.

Student A | Something very strange is happening in the village of Midwich. | ☐

Student B | People collapse if they go too near the village of Midwich. | ☐

Student C | The narrator and his wife are in danger. | ☐

Student D | The army is trying to stop people going to Midwich. | ☐

**b** Write 🖉 just **one** sentence summing up **your understanding** of the key ideas, and the impressions created, in the text.

................................................................................................................................

................................................................................................................................

................................................................................................................................

................................................................................................................................

................................................................................................................................

**c** Look again at the extract on page 2, thinking about the main idea in each paragraph. Does your summary of the whole text include all of those main ideas? If not, change 🖉 your answer to question **1** **b** to make sure it does.

**2** Finally, think about how your impressions changed as you read the extract on page 2. Complete 🖉 these sentences.

In the first paragraph, I got the impression that ..............................................................

................................................................................................................................

................................................................................................................................

................................................................................................................................

When I had finished reading the text, I was left with the impression that ..........................

................................................................................................................................

................................................................................................................................

................................................................................................................................

# Tackling an unseen text

When you tackle an unseen text, aim to:

- read the text very carefully.
- identify the key ideas and information in each paragraph or section of the text.
- think about the writer's purpose and intention: what impressions does the text create?
- check your understanding of the text by summing up its key ideas and information and the impression it creates.
- think about how your impressions change as you read the text; when you have finished reading the text, are your impressions the same as they were when you started reading?

Some of the questions you will face in your exams are designed to test your skill in extracting information from an unseen text. Once you have read and understood the text fully, you are ready to tackle these kinds of question.

Now look at one student's answer to the exam-style question below.

**Exam-style question**

Read again **lines 13 to 19** of the source.

List **four** things from this part of the source about the person that Richard and Janet see in the field. **(4 marks)**

1. He is wearing khaki. ☐

2. He is shouting at them. ☐

3. He is waving a stick. ☐

4. The stick he is waving makes people collapse. ☐

---

A voice **hallooed** at us, away on the left. I looked round and made out a khaki-clad figure in the middle of the next field. He was calling something unintelligible, but the way he was waving his stick was without doubt a sign for us
15  to go back. I stopped.

'Oh, come on, Richard. He's miles away,' said Janet impatiently, and began to run on ahead.

I still hesitated, looking at the figure who was now waving his stick more energetically than ever, and shouting more loudly, though no more intelligibly. I decided to follow Janet. She had perhaps twenty yards start of me by now, and then, just as I started off, she staggered, collapsed without a sound, and lay quite still.

---

**1** Which of this student's answers are correct? Tick ✓ them.

**2** Which of this student's answers are incorrect? Cross them ✗ and write ✐ your own correct answers below.

................................................................................................................................

................................................................................................................................

................................................................................................................................

................................................................................................................................

................................................................................................................................

# Your turn!

After you have read and understood the text, identified its key ideas and the impressions it creates, you are ready to tackle **all of the questions** you are likely to be asked in your exam.

**1** Test your understanding by completing 🖉 the exam-style question below.

**Exam-style question**

Read again **lines 1 to 7** of the source.

List **four** things from this part of the source about the village of Midwich. **(4 marks)**

1. .................................................................................................................................

..................................................................................................................................

..................................................................................................................................

2. ................................................................................................................................

..................................................................................................................................

..................................................................................................................................

3. ................................................................................................................................

..................................................................................................................................

..................................................................................................................................

4. ................................................................................................................................

..................................................................................................................................

..................................................................................................................................

We locked the car, climbed the gate, and started over the field of stubble keeping well in to the hedge. At the end of that we came to another field of stubble and bore leftwards across it, slightly uphill. It was a big field with a good hedge on the far side, and we had to go further left to find a gate we could climb. Half-way across the pasture beyond brought us to the top of the rise, and we were able to look out across Midwich — not that much

5 of it was visible for trees, but we could see a couple of wisps of greyish smoke lazily rising, and the church spire sticking up by the elms. Also, in the middle of the next field I could see four or five cows lying down, apparently asleep.

# Review your skills

## Check up

Review your response to the exam-style question on page 7 and your understanding of the text on page 2. Tick ✓ the column to show how well you think you have done each of the following.

|  | Not quite ✓ | Nearly there ✓ | Got it! ✓ |
|---|---|---|---|
| identified key ideas and information in the text | ☐ | ☐ | ☐ |
| identified the writer's purpose and intention and the impressions the text creates | ☐ | ☐ | ☐ |
| understood the text | ☐ | ☐ | ☐ |

## Need more practice?

Below is another exam-style question, this time relating to source 1 on page 73: an extract from *One Dollar's Worth* by O. Henry. You'll find some suggested points to refer to in the Answers section.

**Before you tackle the question:**

- read the text carefully
- identify the main ideas or information in the text
- think about the purpose of the text and the writer's intentions: what impressions do you get from the text? Do they change as you read it?
- sum up the main ideas in the text and the impressions it creates.

### Exam-style question

Read the first part of the source from **lines 1 to 11**.

List **four** things from this part of the text about Rattlesnake. (4 marks)

How confident do you feel about each of these **skills?** Colour ✐ in the bars.

**1** How do I identify the key ideas in the text?

**2** How do I track the writer's purpose and intention?

**3** How do I know I have understood the text?

**Select and synthesise evidence (AO1)**
**Explain, comment on and analyse how writers use language and structure to achieve effects and influence readers (AO2)**

# ② Analysing a text

This unit will help you analyse a text. The skills you will build are to:

- identify relevant ideas to explore in your analysis
- choose relevant evidence from the text to support ideas
- analyse the writer's choices in the evidence you select.

In the exam, you will face questions like the one below. This is about the source on page 10. This unit will prepare you to write your own response to this question.

**Exam-style question**

You now need to refer **only** to **source A**, from **line 18 to the end**.

How does Mayhew use language to describe his view of London at night time?          **(12 marks)**

The three key questions in the **skills boosts** will help you analyse the text.

**①** How do I begin to analyse a text?          **②** How do I choose evidence?          **③** How do I analyse a quotation?

Read the article on page 10 by Henry Mayhew, first published in *The Illustrated London News* in 1852. You will tackle a 19th-century non-fiction extract in the Reading section of your Paper 2 exam.

## As you read, remember the following: ✓

| Check you understand the focus of the exam-style question you are preparing to respond to. | Think about the ways in which the writer describes London. | Underline or tick any parts of the text which you could use in your response to the question. |
|---|---|---|
| ☐ | ☐ | ☐ |

In 1852, Henry Mayhew went for a ride over London in a hot air balloon. In this newspaper article, he describes the experience.

**Source A** Article from The Illustrated London News, Henry Mayhew

It was late in the evening (a fine autumn one) when the gun was fired that was the signal for the great gas-bag to be loosened from the ropes that held it down to the soil; and immediately the buoyant machine bounded, like a big ball, into the air; and, instantaneously, there was seen a multitude of flat, upturned faces in the gardens below, and some hundreds of outstretched hands fluttering farewell to us.

5  The moment after this, the balloon vaulted over the trees, and we saw the roadway outside the gardens stuck all over with mobs of little people, while the hubbub of the voices below, and the cries of 'Ah bal-loon!' from the boys, rose to the ear like the sound of a distant school let loose to play.

As we floated along above the fields, the sight was the most exquisite visual delight ever experienced. The houses directly underneath us looked like the tiny wooden things out of a child's box of toys, and the streets as if they
10  were ruts in the ground; and we could hear the hum of the voices from every spot we passed over, faint as the buzzing of so many bees.

Far beneath, in the direction we were sailing, lay the suburban fields; and here the earth, with its tiny hills and plains and streams, assumed the appearance of the little coloured plaster models of countries. The roadways striping the land were like narrow brown ribbons, and the river, which we could see winding far away, resembled
15  a long, gray, metallic-looking snake, creeping through the fields. The bridges over the Thames were positively like planks; and the tiny black barges, as they floated along the stream, seemed no bigger than summer insects on the water.

Then, as the dusk of evening descended, and the gas-lights along the different lines of road started into light, one after another, the ground seemed to be covered with little illumination lamps, such as are hung on Christmas-
20  trees.

In the opposite direction lay the **leviathan Metropolis**, with a dense canopy of smoke hanging over it. It was impossible to tell where the monster city began or ended, for the buildings stretched not only to the horizon on either side, but far away into the distance, where, owing to the coming shades of evening and the dense fumes from the million chimneys, the town seemed to blend into the sky, so that there was no distinguishing earth from
25  heaven.

Indeed, it was a most wonderful sight to behold that vast bricken mass of churches and hospitals, banks and prisons, palaces and workhouses, docks and **refuges for the destitute**, parks and squares, and courts and alleys, which make up London—all blent into one immense black spot—to look down upon the whole as the birds of the air look down upon it, and see it dwindled into a mere rubbish heap.

30  Such is the scene we behold, and such the thoughts that stir the brain on contemplating London from the car of a balloon.

leviathan Metropolis: huge city
refuges for the destitute: lodgings for homeless people

# 1 How do I begin to analyse a text?

To begin your analysis, you need to:

* make sure you know what the question is asking you to analyse
* identify relevant ideas you can use in your response to the question.

① Read the exam-style question again.

**Exam-style question**

You now need to refer **only** to **source A**, from **line 18 to the end**.

How does Mayhew use language to describe his view of London at night time? **(12 marks)**

Now look at the first three sentences of the part of the text on page 10 that the question asks you to focus on.

A. ☐ Then, as the dusk of evening descended, and the gas-lights along the different lines of road started into light, one after another, the ground seemed to be covered with little illumination lamps, such as are hung on Christmas-trees.

B. ☐ In the opposite direction lay the leviathan Metropolis, with a dense canopy of smoke hanging over it.

C. ☐ It was impossible to tell where the monster city began or ended, for the buildings stretched not only to the horizon on either side, but far away into the distance, where, owing to the coming shades of evening and the dense fumes from the million chimneys, the town seemed to blend into the sky, so that there was no distinguishing earth from heaven.

a Cross ⊗ any of the sentences above that are not relevant to the question you are answering.

b Which one of the sentences above do you think is most interesting or effective? Tick ✓ it.

You might choose it because you feel the writer has:

* described something particularly vividly
* shown a character's thoughts and feelings very clearly
* made you react strongly to the ideas or events in the text.

Alternatively, there might be another reason why you find it interesting or effective.

c Write ✐ one sentence explaining your choice.

.................................................................................................................................

.................................................................................................................................

.................................................................................................................................

.................................................................................................................................

.................................................................................................................................

.................................................................................................................................

## 2 How do I choose evidence?

When you analyse a text, you need to support your ideas with evidence from the text. Aim to choose short, relevant quotations that will help you answer the question you are responding to.

(1) Read again the exam-style question about the text on page 10.

**Exam-style question**

You now need to refer **only** to **source A**, from **line 18 to the end**.

How does Mayhew use language to describe his view of London at night time?    **(12 marks)**

Now look at one student's response to this question.

> The writer compares the lights of London to Christmas lights: 'Then, as the dusk of evening descended, and the gas-lights along the different lines of road started into light, one after another, the ground seemed to be covered with little illumination lamps, such as are hung on Christmas-trees.'

**a** Which are the most interesting and effective words or phrases in the quotation they use? Circle (A) them.

**b** Which parts of this evidence could you cut to leave a relevant, focused, short quotation? Draw a line (✎) through all the parts of the quotation that are not needed.

(2) Look again at the rest of the text you are being asked to focus on in this exam-style question.

**a** Choose **two** more sentences which you feel are **the most** interesting or effective. Label (✎) them 'A' and 'B' on page 10.

**b** Do you need to use the whole of each of your chosen sentences to answer the question? Circle (A) the most important parts of sentences 'A' and 'B' that you could use as effective, relevant evidence to answer the exam-style question above.

**c** Write (✎) **two** short paragraphs in response to the above question. Begin each paragraph by stating what the writer does in the extract then add the short, relevant quotations you have chosen as evidence to support them.

Paragraph 1: ..................................................................................................................

.............................................................................................................................................

.............................................................................................................................................

.............................................................................................................................................

.............................................................................................................................................

Paragraph 2: ..................................................................................................................

.............................................................................................................................................

.............................................................................................................................................

.............................................................................................................................................

.............................................................................................................................................

# 3 How do I analyse a quotation?

When you analyse a quotation, you need to think about the **effect** of the writer's choices in the quotation and their **impact** on the reader.

(1) Look at the first part of a student's paragraph written in response to a question about the writer's use of language in the extract on page 10.

> The writer compares the lights of London to Christmas lights: 'the ground seemed to be covered with little illumination lamps, such as are hung on Christmas-trees.'

Which of the three pieces of analysis below would make the most effective comment to finish off the paragraph above? Draw (✎) lines linking the notes on the right to the analysis on the left.

A.
> This shows how high the balloon is because the lights look really small.

**Least effective:**
Simply repeats the main point of the paragraph.

B.
> Comparing the lights to Christmas lights makes you think it's a beautiful sight and it reminds you of the happiness of Christmas.

**More effective:**
Comments on the effect of the writer's choices in the quotation.

C.
> This makes me think that the lights of London look like Christmas decorations.

**Most effective:**
Comments on the effect of the writer's choices in the quotation **and** their impact on the reader.

(2) Look at a student's notes on one part of the extract on page 10.

> shows he has a low opinion of the city

> makes it sound small and unimportant

> to look down upon the whole as the birds of the air look down upon it, and see it dwindled into a mere rubbish heap.

> suggests the city is dirty and smelly

> 'mere' makes it sound even less important

Use the student's notes and your own ideas to complete (✎) their paragraph of analysis below. Aim to comment on the effect of the writer's choices and/or their impact on the reader.

> The writer describes looking down on London, saying it looks like 'a mere rubbish heap'.

...................................................................................................................................

...................................................................................................................................

...................................................................................................................................

**Unit 2 Analysing a text**    13

# Analysing a text

To write a good analysis, you need to:

- make sure you know what the question is asking you to do
- identify relevant ideas in the text that will help you answer the question
- select short, relevant quotations to support those ideas
- analyse the writer's choices in those quotations, commenting on their effect and/or their impact on the reader.

Now look at this exam-style question, which you saw at the start of the unit.

**Exam-style question**

You now need to refer **only** to **source A**, from **line 18 to the end**.

How does Mayhew use language to describe his view of London at night time?        (12 marks)

(1) Look at this paragraph from one student's response to the exam-style question above. Link 🖉 the annotations to the paragraph, to show where the student has used each element of a successful paragraph of analysis.

| identifies a relevant idea from the text |
|---|

> The writer describes how polluted London is: 'the dense fumes from the million chimneys'. This shows how polluted London is. The writer says the fumes are 'dense' which helps you imagine how thick and choking they would be, especially when he says 'the million chimneys' which shows how much smoke there would be and how it covered the whole of London. It makes the whole city sound disgusting and dirty.

| comments on the effect of the writer's choices |
|---|

| supports key idea with a quotation from the text |
|---|

| comments on the impact of the writer's choices on the reader |
|---|

(2) How much of this paragraph is **not** effective? Draw a line 🖉 through any parts of the paragraph which:

- are repetitive – they say something that has already been said
- do not help to answer the question.

# Your turn!

You are now going to write 🖉 your own answer in response to the exam-style question.

**Exam-style question**

You now need to refer **only** to **source A**, from **line 18 to the end**.

How does Mayhew use language to describe his view of London at night time?　　　　(12 marks)

1. You will have around 15 minutes in the exam to answer this kind of question so you should aim to write **three** paragraphs. Use these tasks to plan your response:

   a. Look carefully at the lines you are being asked to analyse in the source on page 10.

   b. Choose the **three** sentences from those lines that you find the most interesting and effective and copy 🖉 them in the first row of the table below.

   c. Circle Ⓐ the words, phrases or parts of each sentence that you find the most interesting and effective.

   d. How could you comment on the writer's choices of language in the text you have circled? Note 🖉 some ideas under your chosen sentences in the table below.

| Sentences | | | |
|---|---|---|---|
| Comments | | | |

2. Use your notes above to write 🖉 your response to the exam-style question above on paper.

# Review your skills

## Check up

Review your response to the exam-style question on page 15. Tick ✓ the column to show how well you think you have done each of the following.

|  | Not quite ✓ | Nearly there ✓ | Got it! ✓ |
|---|---|---|---|
| identified relevant ideas | ☐ | ☐ | ☐ |
| selected short, relevant quotations | ☐ | ☐ | ☐ |
| analysed the effect and impact on the reader of the writer's choices | ☐ | ☐ | ☐ |

## Need more practice?

Here is another exam-style question, this time relating to source 2 on page 74: *A letter from the Crimea* by Thomas Monks. You'll find some suggested points to refer to in the Answers section.

### Exam-style question

You now need to refer **only** to **source 2**, from **line 12 to the end**.

How does Thomas Monks use language to describe his life as a soldier?                    **(12 marks)**

How confident do you feel about each of these **skills**? Colour 🖉 in the bars.

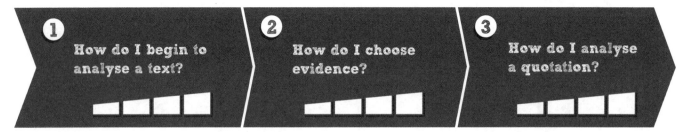

1. **How do I begin to analyse a text?**

2. **How do I choose evidence?**

3. **How do I analyse a quotation?**

# ③ Commenting on words, phrases and language features

This unit will help you comment on language. The skills you will build are to:

- identify significant vocabulary choices in a text
- explore their effect and their impact on the reader
- structure your comments on the writer's vocabulary choices.

In the exam, you will face questions like the one below. This is about the text on page 18. This unit will prepare you to write your own response to this question, focusing on the writer's use of words, phrases and language features. Unit 4 focuses on how to analyse the writer's use of sentence forms.

**Exam-style question**

You now need to refer **only** to **source A**, from **lines 1 to 19**.

How does the writer use language to interest the reader in Ian Fleming and his writing?

(12 marks)

The three key questions in the **skills boosts** will help you comment on language.

| ① How do I start to think about commenting on words, phrases and language features? | ② How do I choose which words, phrases and language features to write about? | ③ How do I comment on the writer's use of words, phrases and language features? |

Read the extract on page 18 from *The Life of Ian Fleming* by John Pearson, published in 1966. You will tackle a 20th-century non-fiction extract in the Reading section of your Paper 2 exam.

## As you read, remember the following:

| Check you understand the focus of the exam question you are preparing to respond to. | Think about how the writer tries to interest the reader in Ian Fleming and his writing. | Mark or underline any language choices in the text which **you** find interesting. |

Just before his first marriage at the age of 43, Ian Fleming wrote the first James Bond novel, *Casino Royale.*

**Source A** The Life of Ian Fleming, John Pearson

James Bond was born at **Goldeneye** on the morning of the third Tuesday of January 1952, when Ian Fleming had just finished breakfast and had ten more weeks of his forty-three years as a bachelor still to run. He had already had his swim out to the reef, and he was wearing white shorts, a coloured beach shirt from Antonio's in Falmouth, and black hide sandals. He came up the steps from the garden while **Violet** was clearing away the remains of

5 breakfast, shut the door of the big living room, closed the **jalousies**, and settled himself down at the brown roll-top desk with his oxidized gold cigarette case, his twenty-year-old **Imperial portable**, and a ream of best quality folio typing paper he had bought at a shop on Madison Avenue ten days earlier.

He had already **appropriated** the name of his hero: James Bond's handbook, *Birds of the West Indies*, was one of the books he liked to keep on his breakfast-table. 'I wanted the simplest, dullest, plainest-sounding name I could

10 find,' he said later. 'James Bond seemed perfect.'

Apart from the name he had no notes and had made no preparations for his story. He simply began to type in his cool, big, shaded room, and for the next seven weeks he kept at it steadily. Every morning between nine and twelve, while **Anne** was in the garden in a large straw hat painting flowers, the sound of the machine echoed through the still house. There were no distractions.

15 Around midday the noise of typing would cease and Fleming would come out of the house and sit yawning and blinking in the strong sunlight by the cliff. He liked to sun himself, usually with his shirt off, before lunch. After he had eaten he slept for an hour or so. At five he returned to his desk to read through what he had written before putting the pages into the blue manilla folder in the bottom left-hand drawer of the desk. By six thirty he was ready for his first real drink of the day.

20 On March 18th, six days before the marriage at Port Maria, the manilla folder was full. Le Chiffre was destroyed and Vesper Lynd was dead as well. Bond had scored his first recorded triumph, and the 62,000 words of one of the strangest thrillers ever written were finished. Probably never before has a book that has sold so well been produced quite so effortlessly...

There were corrections and additions still to be made to the typescript – more with *Casino Royale* than with any of

25 the subsequent books he wrote – and the changes are observable in the first manuscript, which Fleming lovingly preserved and had bound in blue **morocco** and embossed with his initials in gold. There is not a page without its maze of corrections in his strong, forward-sloping handwriting. Many paragraphs have been re-written and pages retyped and pasted in.

Yet it is clear that the whole story was there from the beginning – Bond and his world, the heroine, the casino,

30 the torture scene, the death of the two Bulgars – all came complete as he rattled the story down with such swift assurance at about 2,000 words a day.

**Goldeneye:** Ian Fleming's house in Jamaica
**Violet:** Ian Fleming's housekeeper
**jalousies:** shutters
**Imperial portable:** a typewriter
**appropriated:** borrowed
**Anne:** Fleming's fiancée, later his wife
**morocco:** a fine leather

# 1 How do I start to think about commenting on words, phrases and language features?

Before you can comment on the impact of the writer's use of words, phrases and language features, you need to think about the impact that the text has on **you**.

(1) Re-read the extract on page 18 and think about what the writer is writing about and the impressions the writer gives you of his subject.

**a** Which of the following does the writer write about in the extract? Cross (X) any that are **not** featured in the extract.

A.
☐ Ian Fleming: his personality and lifestyle

B.
☐ How Ian Fleming wrote his novel

C.
☐ The novel, *Casino Royale*

D.
☐ James Bond

E.
☐ Fleming's fiancée, Anne

F.
☐ Fleming's house in Jamaica, Goldeneye

G.
☐ Fleming's housekeeper, Violet

H.
☐ Fleming's childhood

**b** Look again at the things the writer writes about in the extract in part **a**. Which ones does the writer give the most attention, for example, the ones that you get the most information about and the clearest impression of from the text? Choose **three** and tick (✓) them, then write (✏) them in the 'focuses' column of the table below.

**c** Look at your three focuses. Think about the impressions that the text gives you of each one. Note down (✏) **three** words or phrases to sum up the impressions you get of each one from the text.

| The three main focuses of the text are: | The impressions I get of them are: | | |
|---|---|---|---|
| | | | |
| | | | |
| | | | |

## ② How do I choose which words, phrases and language features to write about?

When you have identified the impressions the writer has given you in the text, you need to look more closely at the text to identify the paragraph, then the sentence and then the word or phrase that most strongly created that impression.

① Look at one student's notes on the impression she got of Ian Fleming from the extract on page 18.

> Ian Fleming
> - Likes expensive things – he lives a life of luxury
> - Has a strict routine – he does the same thing every day

**a** Which of the student's impressions above do you get most strongly from the section of the text below? Tick ✓ it.

> He had already had his swim out to the reef, and he was wearing white shorts, a coloured beach shirt from Antonio's in Falmouth, and black hide sandals. He came up the steps from the garden while Violet was clearing away the remains of breakfast, shut the door of the big living room, closed the jalousies, and settled himself down at the brown roll-top desk with his oxidized gold cigarette case, his twenty-year-old Imperial portable, and a ream of best quality folio typing paper he had bought at a shop on Madison Avenue ten days earlier.

**b** Think about the impression of Ian Fleming that you ticked above. Which **sentence** in the section of text gives you that impression most strongly? Underline Ⓐ it.

**c** Which **word or phrase** in the sentence that you have underlined creates that impression most strongly? Circle Ⓐ it.

**d** Write ✏ **one or two** sentences explaining why the word or phrase that you have circled creates that impression.

..............................................................................................................

..............................................................................................................

..............................................................................................................

..............................................................................................................

..............................................................................................................

..............................................................................................................

② Now look closely at lines 29 to 31 in the extract on page 18.

Which **two** words or phrases most strongly give you the impression that Ian Fleming wrote his novel quickly?

..............................................................................................................

..............................................................................................................

## 3 How do I comment on the writer's use of words, phrases and language features?

When you have identified a word or phrase that the writer has used to create a strong impression, you need to comment on **how** that vocabulary choice creates that impression. Think about:

- what that word or phrase **suggests** or **implies**
- what that word or phrase makes you **think** or **feel**.

① Look at the beginning of the extract on page 18.

> James Bond was born at Goldeneye on the morning of the third Tuesday of January 1952

James Bond is a fictional character, created by Ian Fleming. Why do you think the writer of the text chose to use the word born ? What does the word or phrase suggest?

**a** Look at some students' suggestions. Which ones do you agree with? Tick ✓ them.

**Student A** ☐

> It suggests that James Bond is a baby.

**Student B** ☐

> It suggests that Bond was actually born, not just imagined.

**Student C** ☐

> It suggests that Ian Fleming is like a parent who gave birth to James Bond.

**b** Now think about the impact that the word born might have on the reader. Look at some students' suggestions. Which ones do you agree with? Tick ✓ them.

**Student A** ☐

> It makes me think this was an important event.

**Student B** ☐

> It makes me feel that Ian Fleming was a really good writer.

**Student C** ☐

> It makes me feel that James Bond was almost like a real person.

**Student D** ☐

> It makes me think that writing a story is like giving birth to a living thing.

② Now look at the final sentence of the extract on page 18.

> Yet it is clear that the whole story was there from the beginning – Bond and his world, the heroine, the casino, the torture scene, the death of the two Bulgars – all came complete as he rattled the story down with such swift assurance at about 2,000 words a day.

Why do you think the writer chose the word rattled instead of, for example, 'wrote'? Think about:

- what the word suggests or implies about the way Ian Fleming wrote his story
- what the word makes you think or feel about Ian Fleming and his writing.

Write ✎ **one or two** sentences analysing the writer's use of words, phrases and language features in the final sentence above.

......................................................................................................................

......................................................................................................................

......................................................................................................................

**Unit 3 Commenting on words, phrases and language features** 21

# Commenting on words, phrases and language features

To comment on words, phrases and language features successfully, you need to:

- identify the writer's **focus**: what are the key points or ideas in the text?
- think about the **impressions** you get from the text, focusing on those key points or ideas.
- identify the sections of the text, then the sentences, then the **words or phrases** in those sentences that most strongly give you those impressions.
- comment on those words or phrases, thinking about **what they suggest** and **what they make you think or feel**.

Now look at this exam-style question, which you saw at the start of the unit.

**Exam-style question**

You now need to refer **only** to **source A**, from **lines 1 to 19**.

How does the writer use language to interest the reader in Ian Fleming and his writing? **(12 marks)**

(1) Look at this paragraph from one student's response to the question.

identifies a key idea in the text

explains the impression created

comments on what the word or phrase suggests

One way the writer interests the reader is by showing what Ian Fleming was like. The writer creates the impression that Fleming had a strict routine when he wrote his stories. The writer explains that Fleming would write his story 'Every morning between nine and twelve'. The phrase 'every morning' suggests he did the same thing every day which makes me think he was a very organised and determined person.

identifies a word or phrase that creates that impression

uses key words from the question

comments on what the word or phrase makes the reader think or feel

Can you identify the different features of this student's response? Underline (A) the relevant parts of the paragraph, then link (✏) the annotations to them.

# Your turn!

You are now going to write your own answer in response to the exam-style question, focusing on the writer's use of words, phrases and language features. (Unit 4 focuses on how to analyse the writer's use of sentence forms.)

**Exam-style question**

You now need to refer **only** to **source A**, from **lines 1 to 19**.

How does the writer use language to interest the reader in Ian Fleming and his writing? **(12 marks)**

**1** You should aim to write at least **two** paragraphs in response to this question. Use these tasks to complete a planning table like the one below.

**a** Write 🖉 **two** things the writer **focuses** on in **lines 1–19** of the source.

**b** What **impression** does the writer create of each one? 🖉

**c** Identify 🖉 the **word or phrase that most strongly** creates that impression of each one.

**d** Note down 🖉 your ideas about what each word or **phrase suggests or implies**.

**e** Note down 🖉 your ideas about what each word or phrase **makes you think or feel**.

| Writer's focus | Impression created | Strong word or phrase | Suggestion or implication | Effect on reader |
|---|---|---|---|---|
|  |  |  |  |  |
|  |  |  |  |  |

**2** Use your notes to write 🖉 your response to the exam-style question above on paper.

**Unit 3 Commenting on words, phrases and language features**     **23**

# Review your skills

## Check up

Review your response to the exam style question on page 23. Tick ✓ the column to show how well you think you have done each of the following.

|  | Not quite ✓ | Nearly there ✓ | Got it! ✓ |
|---|---|---|---|
| written about the key ideas in the text and the impressions created of them | ☐ | ☐ | ☐ |
| identified words and phrases that help to create those impressions | ☐ | ☐ | ☐ |
| commented on what those words or phrases suggest or imply | ☐ | ☐ | ☐ |
| commented on what those words or phrases make me think or feel | ☐ | ☐ | ☐ |

## Need more practice?

Here is another exam-style question, this time relating to source 3 on page 75: an extract from *Going Commando* by Mark Time. You'll find some suggested points to refer to in the Answers section.

### Exam-style question

You now need to refer **only** to **source 3**, from **line 15 to the end**.

How does the writer use language to describe the experience of training to become a Royal Marine Commando?

(12 marks)

How confident do you feel about each of these **skills?** Colour ✐ in the bars.

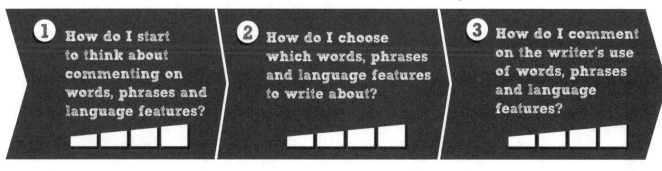

**1** How do I start to think about commenting on words, phrases and language features?

**2** How do I choose which words, phrases and language features to write about?

**3** How do I comment on the writer's use of words, phrases and language features?

Explain, comment on and analyse how writers use language and structure to achieve effects and influence readers (AO2)

# ④ Commenting on sentence forms

This unit will help you comment on sentence forms. The skills you will build are to:

- identify and explore significant choices of sentence form in a text
- build effective comments on the writer's use of sentence forms in a text
- select evidence that will allow you to comment on sentence forms and other language choices.

In the exam, you will face questions like the one below. This is about the text on page 26. This unit will prepare you to write your own response to this question.

**Exam-style question**

You now need to refer **only** to **source A**, from **line 21 to the end**.

How does the writer use language to make you, the reader, understand how he felt when he fell out of the sky?

(12 marks)

The three key questions in the **skills boosts** will help you comment on sentence forms.

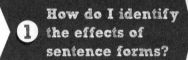
**1** How do I identify the effects of sentence forms?

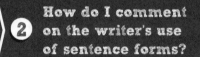
**2** How do I comment on the writer's use of sentence forms?

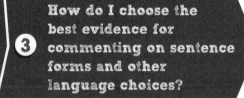
**3** How do I choose the best evidence for commenting on sentence forms and other language choices?

Read the source on page 26: *I Fell Out of the Sky*, an article published in the *Guardian* in 2014. You will tackle a 21st-century non-fiction extract in the Reading section of your Paper 2 exam.

## As you read, remember the following: ✓

Check you understand the focus of the exam question you are preparing to respond to.

Think about how the writer has used sentence forms to describe falling out of the sky.

Mark or underline any sentence forms that you find important in helping you imagine his experience.

In this newspaper article, Neil Laughton describes a terrifying experience.

**Source A** I Fell Out of the Sky, The Guardian

It is not true that your life flashes before your eyes when you're seconds from death. As I hurtled to mine at 60mph, I felt nothing but panic, fear and a deep pang of regret. The earth rushing towards me, I braced for impact. Then the world went black.

Moments earlier I had been on top of the world – soaring and swooping at 50mph like a bird, skimming over lakes,
5 hopping over trees. I was paramotoring – a bit like paragliding, but with a caged engine and propeller strapped to my back. It is a beautiful feeling to be suspended in a floating chair, steering with two cords. At one with the elements, you are defying Newton's laws. It's the ultimate freedom, the ultimate rush.

Paramotoring was a relatively new sport in 2006. My team and I were in Chamonix, in the French Alps, practising for a bid to become the first to fly a paramotor to a record-breaking altitude of over 13,000ft in the Himalayas the
10 following year.

It was Easter Saturday and the plan was to practise stalling and spinning, which involved collapsing and reinflating the canopy at a minimum of 1,000ft. It would prepare us for any emergency on record-attempt day.

After lunch, I volunteered to take off again first from the launch site. The skies were blue and I could see the Alps stretching over the horizon. I had reached only about 100ft and, with a farmhouse in my line of sight, I knew I
15 needed to climb higher to pass it safely. I pulled the brake lines to increase the angle of the wing for extra lift. But I forgot I had tightened them before takeoff and made them far more sensitive. I pulled too hard. That, combined with the **eddies** swirling from the trees and buildings ahead, caused a break in the airflow under the canopy. Instantly, it began to deflate.

I had just enough time to look up and see the thin material of my wing falling towards me like an enormous bunch
20 of useless laundry. I was dropping like a stone.

Tumbling through the air with no way to stop is a sensation of utter helplessness: a truly stomach-churning moment where you know you're not going forwards or upwards; you're just falling. There's no time to think. One second became two, two became three. I closed my eyes. Wallop.

When I came to, I was on my back with cabbage in my mouth. I was lying in a vegetable patch, surrounded by
25 squashed lettuces, broccoli and cabbages. I felt dazed. About 15ft away, I noticed a French family sitting on their patio eating breakfast. Their coffees and croissants halfway to their open mouths, they just sat there staring.

By my left shoulder was a Calor gas canister that, if I had landed on it, could have blown me up. And six inches to my right was an eight-foot steel spike, sharpened at the end. By some incredible twist of good fortune, I'd landed between the two. I couldn't understand how I was still alive. Then I noticed the roof of the farmhouse. It was
30 obliterated, still showering the ground with shattered tiles.

It was the roof that saved my life. The house was 50ft tall and broke my fall. If you throw a tortoise in the air, it will revolve and land on its heaviest element – its shell. The paramotor was my shell, breaking my fall when I hit the roof and then the cabbage patch.

I didn't go to hospital, because incredibly I had no broken bones. I was bruised and shaken but otherwise fine. So I
35 got up, brushed myself down and walked over to apologise to the family, who were rather decent about it, asking only for €500 to repair the roof.

**eddies:** swirling winds that make aircraft very difficult to control

**How do I identify the effects of sentence forms?**

How writers structure their sentences can have a significant impact on your impressions of a text and how it makes you think or feel.

1. One of the key features of sentence form is **sentence length**. Read this extract from the source on page 26 and notice the different sentence lengths.

> But I forgot I had tightened them before takeoff and made them far more sensitive. I pulled too hard. That, combined with the eddies swirling from the trees and buildings ahead, caused a break in the airflow under the canopy. Instantly, it began to deflate.

Now look at some students' comments on the effects created by the structure of the sentences below.

**Student A** — This short sentence adds a feeling of drama to a dramatic mistake the writer made.

**Student B** — This short sentence emphasises how quickly things went wrong.

**Student C** — This longer sentence gives a detailed explanation of what went wrong.

**Student D** — The contrasting length of these two sentences makes the second sentence feel even more dramatic.

a. Which sentences have which effect? Draw lines from the student answers A, B, C and D to the sentences in the extract they match to.

b. Now look at these three sentences from the extract on page 26.

> As I hurtled to mine at 60mph, I felt nothing but panic, fear and a deep pang of regret. The earth rushing towards me, I braced for impact. Then the world went black.

How does the structure of **one, two** or **all three** of these sentences add to your impressions of the writer's experience and your thoughts and feelings about it? Write **one or two** sentences explaining your ideas.

...........................................................................................................................

...........................................................................................................................

...........................................................................................................................

...........................................................................................................................

...........................................................................................................................

...........................................................................................................................

# 2 How do I comment on the writer's use of sentence forms?

When you have identified a significant sentence form, you need to comment on its effect. Think about:
- the impact of the writer's choice of sentence form
- how it adds to your impressions, thoughts and feelings about the text.

① Read this sentence from the extract on page 26.

> I had just enough time to look up and see the thin material of my wing falling towards me like an enormous bunch of useless laundry.

**a** Look at some students' comments on the impact of this part of the text. Tick ✓ the comments you think are effective.

| Student A | Student B | Student C |
|---|---|---|
| This longer sentence is like a pause in the action as the writer watches his parachute collapse and fall towards him. | Using a longer sentence means the writer can describe what he saw in a lot of detail. | Using a longer sentence makes it feel a bit like it is happening in slow motion. |

**b** Now look at some students' comments on how this part of the text adds to their impressions, thoughts and feelings about the text. Tick ✓ the ones that you agree with.

| Student A | Student B | Student C |
|---|---|---|
| Because this sentence is longer and feels slow, it makes the rest of the action seem even faster. | You can imagine how he would feel, knowing what was going to happen next. | It makes it even more tense and dramatic because you're just waiting for him to start falling. |

② Now look at the **next** sentence from the extract.

> I had just enough time to look up and see the thin material of my wing falling towards me like an enormous bunch of useless laundry. I was dropping like a stone.

Write ✐ **one or two** sentences analysing the writer's use of structure in this sentence.
Think about:
- the impact of this short sentence form
- how it adds to your impressions, thoughts and feelings about the text.

......................................................................................................................

......................................................................................................................

......................................................................................................................

......................................................................................................................

......................................................................................................................

## 3 How do I choose the best evidence for commenting on sentence forms and other language choices?

To find the best evidence, you need to focus on parts of the text which create a strong impression, thought or feeling. You can then look closely at those parts of the text for sentence forms and vocabulary choices that you can explore and comment on.

① If you were asked to comment on the writer's use of language in the text on page 26, you could focus on some or all of the following impressions, thoughts and feelings that the writer tries to create.

A. danger and tension     B. adventure and excitement     C. humour

Which of the quotations below contributes strongly to each impression, thought or feeling above? In the first column of boxes, label 🖉 the quotations 'A', 'B' or 'C' – or 'X' if the quotation does not contribute to any of them.

i. ☐ It's the ultimate freedom, the ultimate rush. ☐

ii. ☐ I had just enough time to look up and see the thin material of my wing falling towards me like an enormous bunch of useless laundry. I was dropping like a stone. ☐

iii. ☐ When I came to, I was on my back with cabbage in my mouth. I was lying in a vegetable patch, surrounded by squashed lettuces, broccoli and cabbages. I felt dazed. ☐

② If you wanted to comment on the writer's use of **sentence form** (and how it contributes to the impression the writer creates in the text), which quotation would you choose? Label 🖉 it 'S' in the second column of boxes.

③ If you wanted to comment on the writer's **language choice** (and how it contributes to the impression the writer creates in the text), which quotation would you choose? Label 🖉 it 'L' in the second column of boxes.

④ Look at the quotation you labelled 'S'.

   a Can you find a word or phrase that adds to the impression created in the quotation? Circle Ⓐ it.

   b Write 🖉 **one or two** sentences explaining its effect.

   ................................................................................................................

   ................................................................................................................

   ................................................................................................................

   ................................................................................................................

⑤ Look again at the quotation you labelled 'L'. Does the form of the sentence add to the impression created in the quotation? How? Write 🖉 **one or two** sentences explaining your ideas.

   ................................................................................................................

   ................................................................................................................

   ................................................................................................................

   ................................................................................................................

# Commenting on sentence forms

To write an effective comment on language you need to:

- identify an impression the writer is trying to create in the text
- select a quotation in which that impression is strongly created
- comment on how the writer's choice of words or phrases in the quotation helps to create that impression
- comment on how the writer's use of sentence form in the quotation helps to create that impression.

Now look at the exam-style question which you saw at the start of the unit.

**Exam-style question**

You now need to refer **only** to **source A**, from **line 21 to the end**.

How does the writer use language to make you, the reader, understand how he felt when he fell out of the sky?

(12 marks)

(1) Look at this paragraph from one student's response to the question.

identifies a significant impression created in the text

identifies a significant sentence form

uses key words from the question

> The writer makes the reader understand how he felt by building up the tension as he describes falling to the ground: 'There's no time to think. One second became two, two became three. I closed my eyes. Wallop'. Using short sentences makes it sound like it is happening very quickly and like he is panicking. The last one of these short sentences is just one word 'Wallop'. This word makes you realise how hard he hit the ground and the short sentence makes you realise how everything stopped when he hit it.

comments on how that sentence form adds to the impression created

identifies a significant choice of word or phrase

comments on how that word or phrase adds to the impression created

Can you identify the different features of this student's response? Underline (A) the relevant parts of the paragraph then link (✐) the annotations to them.

# Your turn!

You are now going to write your own answer in response to the exam-style question.

**Exam-style question**

You now need to refer **only** to **source A**, from **line 21 to the end**.

How does the writer use language to make you, the reader, understand how he felt when he fell out of the sky? **(12 marks)**

**1** You should aim to write at least **two** paragraphs in response to this question. Use these tasks to complete the planning table below.

**a** Note down ✐ **two** impressions that the writer is trying to create in **lines 21 to the end** of the article on page 26.

**b** Select ✐ **two** quotations in which those impressions are strongly created. Aim to choose quotations in which the writer's use of words or phrases and sentence forms contributes significantly to the impression created.

**c** Note down ✐ your ideas about the impact of sentence forms in your quotations.

**d** Note down ✐ your ideas about the impact of the writer's use of words and phrases in your quotations.

|  | 1 | 2 |
|---|---|---|
| Impressions created |  |  |
| Quotations |  |  |
| Comment on sentence form |  |  |
| Comment on words or phrases |  |  |

**2** Use your notes to write ✐ your response to the exam-style question above on paper.

# Review your skills

## Check up

Review your response to the exam-style question on page 31. Tick ✓ the column to show how well you think you have done each of the following.

| | Not quite ✓ | Nearly there ✓ | Got it! ✓ |
|---|---|---|---|
| identified two different impressions the writer creates | ☐ | ☐ | ☐ |
| selected relevant quotations | ☐ | ☐ | ☐ |
| commented on the writer's use of sentence forms | ☐ | ☐ | ☐ |
| commented on the writer's use of words and phrases | ☐ | ☐ | ☐ |

Look over all of your work in this chapter. Note down 🖉 the **three** most important things to remember when commenting on sentence forms.

1. ......................................................................................................................

2. ......................................................................................................................

3. ......................................................................................................................

## Need more practice?

Below is another exam-style question, this time relating to source 1 on page 73: an extract from *One Dollar's Worth* by O. Henry. You'll find some suggested points to refer to in the Answers section.

### Exam-style question

Look in detail at **lines 3 to 11** of **source 1**.

How does the writer use language in these lines to show Rattlesnake's thoughts and feelings?

You could include the writer's choice of:
- words and phrases
- language features and techniques
- sentence forms.

(8 marks)

How confident do you feel about each of these **skills**? Colour 🖉 in the bars.

**1** How do I identify the effects of sentence forms?

**2** How do I comment on the writer's use of sentence forms?

**3** How do I choose the best evidence for commenting on sentence forms and other language choices?

**Get started**

**Explain, comment on and analyse how writers use language and structure to achieve effects and influence readers (AO2)**

# ⑤ Commenting on structure

This unit will help you comment on whole text structure. The skills you will build are to:

- identify and explore how the writer has structured a text
- comment on the writer's structural choices.

In the exam, you will face questions like the one below. This is about the text on page 34. This unit will prepare you to write your own response to this question.

## Exam-style question

You need to think about the **whole** of the **source**.

This text is from the opening of a novel.

How has the writer structured the text to interest you as a reader?

You could write about:

- what the writer focuses your attention on at the beginning
- how and why the writer changes this focus as the source develops
- any other structural features that interest you.

(8 marks)

The three key questions in the **skills boosts** will help you comment on structure.

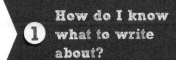
**① How do I know what to write about?**

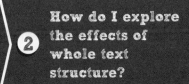
**② How do I explore the effects of whole text structure?**

**③ How do I comment on structure?**

Read the extract on page 34 from *The Unlikely Pilgrimage of Harold Fry* by Rachel Joyce, published in 2013. You will tackle a 20th- or 21st-century fiction extract in the Reading section of your Paper 1 exam.

## As you read, remember the following: ✓

Check you understand the focus of the exam question you are preparing to respond to.

Think about the ways in which the writer has structured the opening of the novel.

Mark or underline any parts of the text which **you** find interesting.

This extract is from the opening of a novel.

**Source A** The Unlikely Pilgrimage of Harold Fry, Rachel Joyce

The letter that would change everything arrived on a Tuesday. It was an ordinary morning in mid-April that smelled of clean washing and grass cuttings. Harold Fry sat at the breakfast table, freshly shaved, in a clean shirt and tie, with a slice of toast that he wasn't eating. He gazed beyond the kitchen window at the clipped lawn, which was spiked in the middle by Maureen's telescopic washing line, and trapped on all three sides by the neighbours'
5   stockade fencing.

'Harold!', called Maureen above the vacuum cleaner. 'Post!'

He thought he might like to go out, but the only thing to do was mow the lawn and he had done that yesterday. The vacuum tumbled into silence, and his wife appeared, looking cross, with a letter. She sat opposite Harold.

Maureen was a slight woman with a cap of silver hair and a brisk walk. When they first met, nothing had pleased
10   him more than to make her laugh. To watch her neat frame collapse into unruly happiness. 'It's for you,' she said. He didn't know what she meant until she slid an envelope across the table, and stopped it just short of Harold's elbow. They both looked at the letter as if they had never seen one before. It was pink. 'The postmark says Berwick-upon-Tweed.'

He didn't know anyone in Berwick. He didn't know many people anywhere. 'Maybe it's a mistake.'

15   'I think not. They don't get something like a postmark wrong.' She took toast from the rack. She liked it cold and crisp.

Harold studied the mysterious envelope. Its pink was not the color of the bathroom suite, or the matching towels and fluffed cover for the toilet seat. That was a vivid shade that made Harold feel he shouldn't be there. But this was delicate. A Turkish Delight pink. His name and address were scribbled in ballpoint, the clumsy
20   letters collapsing into one another as if a child had dashed them off in a hurry: Mr. H. Fry, 13 Fossebridge Road, Kingsbridge, South Hams. He didn't recognise the handwriting.

'Well?' said Maureen, passing a knife. He held it to the corner of the envelope, and tugged it through the fold. 'Careful,' she warned.

He could feel her eyes on him as he eased out the letter, and prodded back his reading glasses. The page was
25   typed, and addressed from a place he didn't know: St. Bernadine's Hospice. Dear Harold, This may come to you as some surprise. His eyes ran to the bottom of the page.

'Well?' said Maureen again.

'Good lord. It's from Queenie Hennessy.'

Maureen speared a nugget of butter with her knife and flattened it the length of her toast. 'Queenie who?'

30   'She worked at the brewery. Years ago. Don't you remember?'

Maureen shrugged. 'I don't see why I should. I don't know why I'd remember someone from years ago. Could you pass the jam?'

He'd said the same thing about next door's cat. It disappeared years ago, and no one has seen it since.

# How do I know what to write about?

In the opening of a novel, the writer always aims to get you interested in the story they are about to tell. You need to work out which key elements of the story are the most interesting or significant.

1. The key story elements in the opening of a novel often include:

characters | the people you are introduced to in the extract

relationships | how those characters relate to each other

events | what happens in the extract

setting | the place where these events happen

**a** In the extract on page 34, you are introduced to three **characters**.

Harold Fry ☐   Maureen Fry ☐   Queenie Hennessy ☐

Which character do you learn most about in this extract? Tick ✓ your choice then write ✐ **one or two** sentences explaining why you chose it.

..................................................................................................................................

..................................................................................................................................

..................................................................................................................................

..................................................................................................................................

**b** Which **relationship** between the characters do you learn most about in the extract?

Harold and Maureen ☐   Maureen and Queenie ☐   Harold and Queenie ☐

Tick ✓ your choice, then write ✐ **one or two** sentences explaining why you chose it.

..................................................................................................................................

..................................................................................................................................

..................................................................................................................................

..................................................................................................................................

**c** There are two **events** in the extract on page 34.

Breakfast ☐   Harold gets a letter ☐

Which event do you think is the most important or significant in this extract? Tick ✓ your choice, then write ✐ **one or two** sentences explaining why you chose it.

..................................................................................................................................

..................................................................................................................................

..................................................................................................................................

..................................................................................................................................

## 2 How do I explore the effects of whole text structure?

When you have identified some important features of whole text structure, you can begin to explore them, thinking about how the writer has tried to make them interesting or significant.

1 Look at the quotations below, taken from the extract on page 34. Each one tells you something significant.

Label each one 'C', 'R', 'E', 'S' or 'N' in the first column of boxes, to indicate if it tells you something significant about a **C**haracter, a **R**elationship, an **E**vent, a **S**etting or **N**one of these.

i. The letter that would change everything arrived on a Tuesday.

ii. He thought he might like to go out, but the only thing to do was mow the lawn and he had done that yesterday.

iii. Maureen was a slight woman with a cap of silver hair and a brisk walk. When they first met, nothing had pleased him more than to make her laugh.

iv. Harold studied the mysterious envelope. Its pink was not the colour of the bathroom suite, or the matching towels and fluffed cover for the toilet seat.

v. The page was typed, and addressed from a place he didn't know: St. Bernadine's Hospice. Dear Harold, This may come to you as some surprise. His eyes ran to the bottom of the page.

vi. 'Good lord. It's from Queenie Hennessy.'

2 Which of the quotations above reveal the most interesting or significant ideas?

a Choose **three** and number them 1, 2 and 3 in the second column of tick boxes.

b Write **one or two** sentences explaining what you find interesting or significant in each numbered quotation and what it reveals about the character or relationship, setting or event in the extract on page 34.

1. ....................................................................................................................................

....................................................................................................................................

....................................................................................................................................

2. ....................................................................................................................................

....................................................................................................................................

....................................................................................................................................

3. ....................................................................................................................................

....................................................................................................................................

....................................................................................................................................

## ③ How do I comment on structure?

Comments on structure can focus on:
- what the writer has done in the extract
- how the writer has done it
- its impact on the reader.

① Look at this exam-style question.

**Exam-style question**

How has the writer structured the text to interest you as a reader?

Now look at the beginning of a paragraph from one student's response to the question.

> The writer interests the reader by introducing a failing relationship in the opening of the novel: 'When they first met, nothing had pleased him more than to make her laugh.'

**a** Look at the next part of this student's paragraph in which she comments on **how the writer has done that**. Which comments do you agree with? Tick ✓ them.

This makes me think she does not laugh any more and he does not care. ☐

Maureen seems quite angry and Harold seems bored and neither of them laugh at all. ☐

It suggests the relationship between Harold and Maureen is not as good as it used to be. ☐

**b** Look at the final part of this student's paragraph in which she comments on **the impact of the writer's choices on the reader.** Which comments do you agree with? Tick ✓ them.

This is interesting because you want to see how these characters and their relationship develop. ☐

It makes you feel sorry for Harold and you want to find out if his life gets any better or more exciting. ☐

It makes you think the story might be about them saving their marriage so you want to find out if they do. ☐

② Now look at the beginning of another student's response to the exam-style question above. Write 🖉 **one or two** sentences to finish the paragraph, thinking about:
- **how** the writer has grabbed the reader's attention
- the **impact** this opening sentence might have on the reader.

The opening sentence of the novel grabs the reader's attention immediately: 'The letter that would change everything arrived on a Tuesday.'

..................................................................................................................

..................................................................................................................

..................................................................................................................

..................................................................................................................

# Commenting on structure

To write an effective comment on structure, you need to:
- identify a feature of the text's structure
- comment on what the writer has done in that feature
- comment on how the writer has achieved it
- comment on its impact on the reader.

Now look at the exam-style question about source A on page 34, which you saw at the start of the unit.

**Exam-style question**

You need to think about the **whole** of the **source**.

This text is from the opening of a novel.

How has the writer structured the text to interest you as a reader?

You could write about:
- what the writer focuses your attention on at the beginning
- how and why the writer changes this focus as the source develops
- any other structural features that interest you.

(8 marks)

(1) Look at a paragraph written by one student in response to the exam-style question above.

identifies a feature of the text's structure

uses key words from the question

comments on what the writer has done in that feature

> The writer has structured the text to focus the reader's attention on the letter from the beginning and then makes it sound very mysterious. 'They both looked at the letter as if they had never seen one before.' This makes me think Harold and Maureen never get letters so this must be something special or strange. It's also pink and Harold doesn't recognise the writing on it so it suggests that the letter inside will be something exciting and unexpected. You really want to find out who the letter is from and why they are writing to Harold and how it will change everything.

comments on how the writer has achieved that feature's effect

comments on its impact on the reader

Can you identify all the different things the student has included in this paragraph? Link 🖉 the annotations to the paragraph to show where the student has included them.

# Your turn!

You are now going to write 🖉 your own answer in response to the exam-style question about source A on page 34.

**Exam-style question**

You need to think about the **whole** of the **source**.

This text is from the opening of a novel.

How has the writer structured the text to interest you as a reader?

You could write about:

- what the writer focuses your attention on at the beginning
- how and why the writer changes this focus as the source develops
- any other structural features that interest you.

(8 marks)

① You should aim to write at least **two** paragraphs in response to this question. Use these tasks to complete the planning table below.

a Note down 🖉 **two** significant features of the **whole text structure** of the extract.

b Choose 🖉 a quotation to support each of those features.

c Note down 🖉 your ideas about what the writer has done in each feature.

d Note down 🖉 your ideas about how the writer has achieved it.

e Note down 🖉 your ideas about the impact of each feature on the reader.

|  | 1 | 2 |
|---|---|---|
| Significant features |  |  |
| Quotation |  |  |
| What the writer has done |  |  |
| How the writer has done that |  |  |
| Its impact on the reader |  |  |

② Use your notes to write 🖉 your response to the exam-style question above on paper.

# Review your skills

## Check up

Review your response to the exam-style question on page 39. Tick ✓ the column to show how well you think you have done each of the following.

|  | Not quite ✓ | Nearly there ✓ | Got it! ✓ |
|---|---|---|---|
| identified what to write about | ☐ | ☐ | ☐ |
| explored the effect of whole text structure | ☐ | ☐ | ☐ |
| commented on structure | ☐ | ☐ | ☐ |

## Need more practice?

Below is another exam-style question, this time relating to source 1 on page 73: an extract from *One Dollar's Worth* by O. Henry. You'll find some suggested points to refer to in the Answers section.

### Exam-style question

You need to think about the **whole** of the **source**.

This text is from the opening of a short story.

How has the writer structured the text to interest you as a reader?

You could write about:

- what the writer focuses your attention on at the beginning
- how and why the writer changes this focus as the source develops
- any other structural features that interest you.

(8 marks)

How confident do you feel about each of these **skills?** Colour 🖉 in the bars.

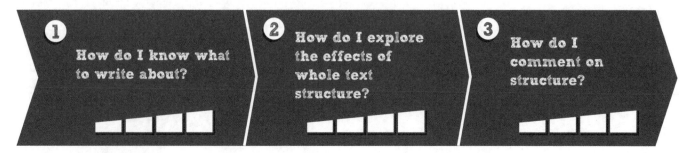

**1** How do I know what to write about?

**2** How do I explore the effects of whole text structure?

**3** How do I comment on structure?

# ⑥ Evaluating a text

This unit will help you evaluate a text. The skills you will build are to:

- recognise the writer's intentions
- identify where in the text the writer has attempted to achieve that intention
- comment on how the writer has achieved that intention
- write an evaluation.

In the exam, you will face questions like the one below. This is about the text on page 42. This unit will prepare you to write your own response to this question.

This is about the text on page 42.

**Exam-style question**

Focus this part of your answer on the second half of the source, from **line 18 to the end**.

A student, having read this section of the text, said: 'The writer makes you wonder what has happened to Harry Pope in this part of the text. When you find out about the snake, it's a real shock.'

To what extent do you agree?

In your response, you could:

- write about your own impressions of the narrator's thoughts and feelings
- evaluate how the writer has created these impressions
- support your opinions with quotations from the text.                  **(20 marks)**

The three key questions in the **skills boosts** will help you evaluate texts.

**1** How do I identify where the writer has tried to achieve their intention?  **2** How do I comment on the writer's intention?  **3** How do I evaluate the writer's success?

Read the extract on page 42 from *Poison*, a short story by Roald Dahl published in 1950. You will tackle a 20th- or 21st-century fiction extract in the Reading section of your Paper 1 exam.

Read the extract on page 42

## As you read, remember the following: ⊘

Check you understand the focus of the exam question you are preparing to respond to.

Mark or highlight any parts of the text relevant to the question you are going to answer: where the writer makes you wonder what is happening.

This is the opening of a short story set in India in the first half of the 20th century.

**Source A** Poison, Roald Dahl

It must have been around midnight when I drove home, and as I approached the gates of the bungalow, I switched off the headlamps of the car so the beam wouldn't swing in through the window of the side bedroom and wake Harry Pope. But I needn't have bothered. Coming up the drive I noticed his light was still on, so he was awake anyway – unless perhaps he'd dropped off while reading.

5 I parked the car and went up the five steps to the balcony, counting each step carefully in the dark so I wouldn't take an extra one which wasn't there when I got to the top. I crossed the balcony, pushed through the screen doors into the house itself and switched on the light in the hall. I went across to the door of Harry's room, opened it quietly, and looked in.

He was lying on the bed and I could see he was awake. But he didn't move. He didn't even turn his head towards 10 me, but I heard him say, 'Timber, Timber, come here.'

He spoke slowly, whispering each word carefully, separately, and I pushed the door right open and started to go quickly across the room.

'Stop. Wait a moment, Timber.' I could hardly hear what he was saying. He seemed to be straining enormously to get the words out.

15 'What's the matter, Harry?'

'Sshhh!' he whispered. 'Sshhh! For God's sake don't make a noise. Take your shoes off before you come nearer. *Please* do as I say, Timber.'

The way he was speaking reminded me of George Barling after he got shot in the stomach when he stood leaning against a crate containing a spare aeroplane engine, holding both hands on his stomach and saying things about 20 the German pilot in just the same hoarse straining half whisper Harry was using now.

'Quickly, Timber, but take your shoes off first.'

I couldn't understand about taking off the shoes but I figured that if he was as ill as he sounded I'd better humour him, so I bent down and removed the shoes and left them in the middle of the floor. Then I went over to his bed.

'Don't touch the bed! For God's sake don't touch the bed!' He was still speaking like he'd been shot in the stomach 25 and I could see him lying there on his back with a single sheet covering three-quarters of his body. He was wearing a pair of pyjamas with blue, brown, and white stripes, and he was sweating terribly. It was a hot night and I was sweating a little myself, but not like Harry. His whole face was wet and the pillow around his head was sodden with moisture. It looked like a bad **go of malaria** to me.

'What is it, Harry?'

30 'A **krait**,' he said.

'A *krait*! Oh, my God! Where'd it bite you? How long ago?'

'Shut up,' he whispered.

'Listen, Harry,' I said, and I leaned forward and touched his shoulder. 'We've got to be quick. Come on now, quickly, tell me where it bit you.' He was lying there very still and tense as though he was holding on to himself hard 35 because of sharp pain.

'I haven't been bitten,' he whispered, 'Not yet. It's on my stomach. Lying there asleep.'

**go of malaria:** case of malaria, a tropical disease spread by mosquitoes; symptoms include fever and vomiting

**krait:** a poisonous snake

# 1 How do I identify where the writer has tried to achieve their intention?

In every text, the writer has an intention: the impact they want their text to have on the reader. To evaluate a text, you need to focus on the **writer's intention** and identify **where in the text the writer has achieved it.**

① The question you are going to answer gives you one student's ideas about the writer's intention:

**Exam-style question**

'The writer makes you wonder what has happened to Harry Pope in this part of the text. When you find out about the snake, it's a real shock.'

To respond to this question, you need to work out where in the text **the writer makes you wonder what has happened to Harry Pope.** Look at some of the things we are told about Harry.

A. ☐ 'Sshhh!' he whispered. 'Sshhh! For God's sake don't make a noise. Take your shoes off before you come nearer. *Please* do as I say Timber.'

B. ☐ 'Quickly, Timber, but take your shoes off first.'

C. ☐ 'Don't touch the bed! For God's sake don't touch the bed!' He was still speaking like he'd been shot in the stomach …

D. ☐ His whole face was wet and the pillow around his head was sodden with moisture.

Which ones make you think that something has happened to Harry Pope? Tick ✓ them.

② Look closely again at the extract. Which of the following does the narrator, Timber, think *might* have happened to Harry Pope? Tick ✓ them.

| A. | He has been shot | ☐ | B. | He has been bitten by a snake | ☐ |
| C. | He has malaria | ☐ | D. | He suffers from heart problems | ☐ |
| E. | He has heat sickness | ☐ | F. | He is playing a joke on Timber | ☐ |

③ Write ✏ **one or two** sentences summing up:

• how the writer tries to make you wonder what has happened to Harry Pope

• why the ending of the extract is a surprise.

..............................................................................................................................

..............................................................................................................................

..............................................................................................................................

④ Look again at the extract from the exam-style question in question ①. Do you agree with this student's point of view? Tick ✓ **one** of the boxes below to show how strongly you agree.

| Yes, completely | ☐ | No, not at all | ☐ | I partly agree | ☐ |

# 2  How do I comment on the writer's intention?

The best comments on the writer's intention do not simply say what the writer has done in the text: they comment on how the writer's choices help them to achieve their intention.

**①** The question you are going to answer focuses on how the writer makes you wonder what has happened to Harry Pope.

Look at these sentences from the text on page 42.

> 'Sshhh!' he whispered. 'Sshhh! For God's sake don't make a noise. Take your shoes off before you come nearer. *Please* do as I say Timber.'

Which words and phrases in these sentences strongly suggest that something is wrong with Harry Pope? Circle (A) them.

**②** Now look at one student's comments on this part of the text.

| | |
|---|---|
| Everything Harry says in this quotation makes him sound desperate. | This makes you wonder what has happened to him. |
| He uses the phrase 'For God's sake'. | This makes him sound even more desperate. |
| The word 'please' is in italics to show how he emphasises it. | It makes Harry sound like he is begging the narrator. |

**a** Which comments explain **what the writer has done** in the text? Label (✎) them **W**.

**b** Which comments explain **how this helps the writer achieve his intention** of suggesting that something has happened to Harry Pope? Label (✎) them **H**.

**c** Which comments do neither? Cross (✗) them.

**③** Now look at these sentences from the text on page 42.

> 'Don't touch the bed! For God's sake don't touch the bed!' He was still speaking like he'd been shot in the stomach

**a** Which words and phrases in these sentences strongly suggest that something is wrong with Harry Pope? Circle (A) them.

**b** Write (✎) **one or two** sentences commenting on **what the writer has done** in the sentences above and **how it makes you wonder what has happened to Harry Pope.**

.................................................................................................................

.................................................................................................................

.................................................................................................................

.................................................................................................................

.................................................................................................................

.................................................................................................................

.................................................................................................................

# 3  How do I evaluate the writer's success?

To evaluate the success of a text, you need to comment on **how well** the writer has done what they set out to do: whether they have **achieved their intention**.

① Look at the beginning of a paragraph evaluating how successfully the writer makes you wonder what has happened to Harry Pope.

> The writer shows how shocked the narrator is when he hears about the snake: 'A krait! Oh, my God! Where'd it bite you? How long ago?'

**a** You are going to build an effective comment to complete the paragraph.
Choose and tick ✓:

- **one** comment on what the writer has done
- **one** comment on how this helps the writer's intention
- **one** comment that evaluates how successfully it creates the writer's intended impact on the reader.

**What has the writer done?**

| The narrator speaks in very short sentences. ☐☐ | The narrator uses the phrase 'Oh, my God'. ☐☐ | The narrator uses lots of exclamations and asks lots of questions. ☐☐ |

**How does it help the writer's intention?**

| This makes the narrator sound like he is panicking. ☐☐ | It suggests the narrator is shocked. ☐☐ | It suggests that he cannot believe what is going on. ☐☐ |

**Is it successful?**

| The writer is building up the tension very powerfully as you realise how serious the snake bite could be. ☐☐ | This really makes you think Harry has been bitten and it makes what has actually happened more of a surprise. ☐☐ | The writer is very successfully making the situation more and more dramatic as you feel like everything is happening really quickly and the situation is out of control. ☐☐ |

**b** In what order would you sequence your three chosen sentences in your paragraph? Number ✏ them.

**c** Read through and write ✏ your chosen sentences on paper in your chosen order to make sure that they effectively comment on and evaluate the writer's choices.

# Evaluating a text

To write a good evaluation, you need to:

- identify the writer's intention
- identify where in the text the writer has attempted to achieve their intention
- comment on what the writer has done and how it helps them to achieve their intention
- comment on the success of its impact on the reader.

Now look at the exam-style question about source A on page 42, which you saw at the start of the unit.

**Exam-style question**

Focus this part of your answer on the second half of the source, from **line 18 to the end**.

A student, having read this section of the text said: 'The writer makes you wonder what has happened to Harry Pope in this part of the text. When you find out about the snake, it's a real shock.'

To what extent do you agree?

In your response, you could:

- write about your own impressions of the narrator's thoughts and feelings
- evaluate how the writer has created these impressions
- support your opinions with quotations from the text. (20 marks)

(1) Look at a paragraph written by one student in response to the exam-style question above.

| identifies where the writer has tried to achieve their intention |
|---|

> Just before you find out what has actually happened, the narrator describes Harry Pope: 'He was lying there very still and tense as though he was holding on to himself hard because of sharp pain.' The writer makes you think he has been bitten by the snake and is dying in agony by describing how hard he is holding himself and the pain as sharp. This is very dramatic but the story becomes really tense when you find out the snake is still there and could bite him at any minute.

| comments on how what the writer has done helps the writer's intention |
|---|

| comments on what the writer has done |
|---|

| comments on the success of its impact on the reader |
|---|

Can you identify all the different things the student has included in this paragraph? Link ✏ the annotations to the paragraph to show where the student has included them.

# Your turn!

You are now going to write your own answer in response to the exam-style question.

**Exam-style question**

Focus this part of your answer on the second half of the source, from **line 18 to the end**.

A student, having read this section of the text said: 'The writer makes you wonder what has happened to Harry Pope in this part of the text. When you find out about the snake, it's a real shock.'

To what extent do you agree?

In your response, you could:

- write about your own impressions of the narrator's thoughts and feelings
- evaluate how the writer has created these impressions
- support your opinions with quotations from the text. **(20 marks)**

**1** You should aim to write at least **three** paragraphs in response to this question. Use these tasks to complete the planning table below.

**a** Note down ✏ **three points in the text** where the writer has made you wonder what has happened to Harry Pope.

**b** Choose ✏ **one** quotation to support **each** of those points.

**c** Note down ✏ your ideas about what the writer has done in each quotation.

**d** Note down ✏ your ideas about how this helps the writer to achieve his intention.

**e** Note down ✏ your ideas about its impact on the reader and how successful this is.

|  | 1 | 2 | 3 |
|---|---|---|---|
| Points |  |  |  |
| Quotations |  |  |  |
| What has the writer done? |  |  |  |
| How? |  |  |  |
| Is it successful? |  |  |  |

# Review your skills

## Check up

Review your response to the exam-style question on page 47. Tick ✓ the column to show how well you think you have done each of the following.

|  | Not quite ✓ | Nearly there ✓ | Got it! ✓ |
|---|---|---|---|
| identified where the writer has tried to achieve their intention | ☐ | ☐ | ☐ |
| commented on the writer's intention | ☐ | ☐ | ☐ |
| evaluated the writer's success | ☐ | ☐ | ☐ |

## Need more practice?

Here is another exam-style question, this time relating to source 1 on page 73: an extract from *One Dollar's Worth* by O. Henry. You'll find some suggested points to refer to in the Answers section.

### Exam-style question

Focus this part of your answer on the first half of the source, from **lines 1 to 22**.

A student, having read this section of the text, said: 'The writer grabs your attention with the threatening letter. You almost want Rattlesnake to take revenge on Judge Derwent.'

To what extent do you agree?

In your response, you could:

- write about your own impressions of Rattlesnake and Judge Derwent
- evaluate how the writer has created these impressions
- support your opinions with quotations from the text.

(20 marks)

How confident do you feel about each of these **skills?** Colour ✏ in the bars.

1 How do I identify where the writer has tried to achieve their intention?

2 How do I comment on the writer's intention?

3 How do I evaluate the writer's success?

# (7) Synthesising and comparing

This unit will help you synthesise and compare information and ideas from two different sources. The skills you will build are to:

- identify relevant information in each source
- identify similarities in the key ideas and information in the two sources
- write a comparison of the key ideas and information in two sources.

In the exam, you will face questions like the one below. This is about the sources on page 50. This unit will prepare you to write your own response to this question.

**Exam-style question**

You need to refer to **source A** and **source B** for this question.

Use details from **both** sources. Write a summary of the differences between the writers' experiences of going to bed.

(8 marks)

The three key questions in the **skills boosts** will help you synthesise and compare similarities or differences in two texts.

**1** How do I identify points of comparison?

**2** How do I synthesise information and ideas in two sources?

**3** How do I write a comparison?

Read the extracts on page 50 from *London Labour and the London Poor* by Henry Mayhew, published in four volumes between 1851 and 1861, and *The Life and Times of the Thunderbolt Kid* by Bill Bryson, published in 2006. You will tackle one 19th-century and one 20th- or 21st-century non-fiction extract in the Reading section of your Paper 2 exam.

## As you read, remember the following:

 Check you understand the focus of the exam question you are preparing to respond to.

 Mark or highlight any ideas and information in each source that is relevant to the exam question.

 Consider any similarities or differences in the ideas and information in each source.

Lodging houses were provided for homeless people in Victorian Britain. Here the journalist Henry Mayhew records one man's description of them.

**Source A** London Labour and the London Poor, Henry Mayhew

In the room where I slept, which was like a barn in size, the tiles were off the roof, and as there was no ceiling, I could see the blue sky from where I lay. For the bed with the view of the blue sky I paid 3d. If it rained there was no shelter.

5    I have slept in a room in Brick-lane, Whitechapel, in which were fourteen beds. In the next bed to me, on the one side, was a man, his wife, and three children, and a man and his wife on the other. All the beds were occupied, single men being mixed with the married couples. The question is never asked, when a man and woman go to a lodging-house, if they are man and wife. All must pay before they go to bed, or be turned into the street. These beds were made – as all the low lodging-house beds are – of the worst **cotton flocks** stuffed in coarse, strong canvas. There is a pair of sheets, a blanket, and a rug. I have known the bedding to be unchanged for three

10   months; but that is not general. The beds are an average size. Dirt is the rule with them, and cleanliness the exception. They are all infested with **vermin**. I never met with an exception. No one is required to wash before going to bed in any of these places (except at a very few, where a very dirty fellow would not be admitted), unless he has been walking on a wet day without shoes or stockings, and then he must bathe his feet.

Bill Bryson remembers staying at his grandparents' house as a child.

**Source B** The Life and Times of the Thunderbolt Kid, Bill Bryson

The sleeping porch was a slightly rickety, loosely enclosed porch on the back of the house that was only **notionally** separate from the outside world. It contained an ancient sagging bed that my grandfather slept in in the summer when the house was uncomfortably warm. But sometimes in the winter when the house was full of guests it was pressed into service, too.

5    The only heat in the sleeping porch was that of any human being who happened to be out there. It couldn't have been more than one or two degrees warmer than the world outside – and outside was perishing. So to sleep on the sleeping porch required preparation. First, you put on long underwear, pajamas, jeans, a sweatshirt, your grandfather's old cardigan and bathrobe, two pairs of woolen socks on your feet and another on your hands, and a hat with earflaps tied beneath the chin. Then you climbed into bed and were immediately covered with a dozen

10   bed blankets, three horse blankets, all the household overcoats, a canvas tarpaulin, and a piece of old carpet. I'm not sure that they didn't lay an old wardrobe on top of that, just to hold everything down. It was like sleeping under a dead horse. For the first minute or so it was unimaginably cold, shockingly cold, but gradually your body heat seeped in and you became warm and happy in a way you would not have believed possible only a minute or two before. It was bliss.

**cotton flocks**: a cheap filling for mattresses, often lumpy and uncomfortable
**vermin**: parasites, bed bugs
**notionally**: in theory, not in reality

# 1 How do I identify points of comparison?

To identify key points for comparison, you need to identify the key ideas and information in the two sources that are relevant to the task you are tackling.

① Look at this exam-style question.

**Exam-style question**

Use details from **both** sources. Write a summary of the differences between the writers' experiences of going to bed.

Now look at one student's notes identifying key ideas and information in the **first half** of each source.

**Source A:** *London Labour and the London Poor*

A. | The roof is full of holes. | ☐

B. | You have to share a room with lots of other people. | ☐

C. | You have to pay or you get thrown out. | ☐

D. | The beds sound uncomfortable. | ☐

E. ........................................................................... ☐

F. ........................................................................... ☐

G. ........................................................................... ☐

**Source B:** *The Life and Times of the Thunderbolt Kid*

A. | He is sleeping in a porch on the back of the house. | ☐

B. | His grandfather slept in the bed on the porch when it was too hot in the house. | ☐

C. | Sometimes the bed in the porch is used for guests. | ☐

D. | The bed is ancient and sagging. | ☐

E. | The porch is freezing cold. | ☐

F. ........................................................................... ☐

G. ........................................................................... ☐

H. ........................................................................... ☐

a Which key ideas do **not** focus on the writers' experiences of going to bed and are therefore **not** relevant to the question? Cross ⊗ them.

b Look again at source **A** on page 50. Complete ✎ the student's notes above, noting down all the key ideas and information in the **second half** of the source. Cross ⊗ any that are not relevant to the exam-style question.

c Look again at source **B** on page 50. Complete ✎ the student's notes above, noting down all the key ideas and information in the **second half** of the source. Cross ⊗ any that are not relevant to the exam-style question.

## 2 How do I synthesise information and ideas in two sources?

When you synthesise information from sources in order to compare their differences:

- **don't** look for **completely different** ideas
- **do** look for ideas that are **related but different**.

① Look at one student's notes identifying the key ideas and information from source B, and giving a brief summary of those key ideas.

> *Source B: The Life and Times of the Thunderbolt Kid*
> - *He is sleeping in a porch on the back of the house.*
> - *The bed is ancient and sagging.*
> - *The porch is freezing cold.*
> - *The writer puts on layers and layers of clothing to try to keep warm.*
> - *The writer then has blankets, coats and a carpet put on him. It's like 'sleeping under a dead horse'.*
> - *At first it is freezing but he soon warms up.*

> *Source B Summary*
> *The writer writes about:*
> - *the mattress*
> - *the temperature*
> - *discomfort*
> - *clothing and blankets*
> - *warmth and comfort.*

Now look at the student's notes on the key ideas and information in source A.
Use them to write  a brief summary of those key ideas.

> *Source A: London Labour and the London Poor*
> - *The roof is full of holes.*
> - *You have to share a room with lots of other people.*
> - *You have to pay or you get thrown out.*
> - *The beds sound uncomfortable.*
> - *The bedding is not washed very often.*
> - *The beds are infested with vermin.*
> - *None of the people who sleep there have to wash.*

> *Source A Summary*
> *The writer writes about:*
> - .......................................................
> - .......................................................
> - .......................................................
> - .......................................................
> - .......................................................

② Compare the student's summary of source B with your summary of source A.
What **differences** can you spot? Complete the sentence below, summing up **one** of the differences in the sources.

In source A, the writer focuses on ............................................................................

.......................................................................................................................

.......................................................................................................................

whereas in source B the writer focuses on ...........................................................

.......................................................................................................................

.......................................................................................................................

## 3 How do I write a comparison?

A comparison should identify significant similarities and/or differences in the key ideas and information in the two sources, and support them using evidence from each source.

① Each comparison you make between two sources should be clearly stated at the start of the paragraph. For example:

> Both writers complain about the situation they have to sleep in but they complain about different things.

**a** Choose **one** relevant quotation from **each** source to support this point. Write ✐ them below.

Source A

Source B

**b** Choose **two** key details from **each** of your quotations. Use them to complete ✐ the sentences below.

In source A, the writer describes

In source A, the writer describes

**c** You may need to explain the significance of your evidence from each source. Complete ✐ the sentences below.

This gives the impression that

This suggests

# Synthesising and comparing

To write a good comparison of the key ideas and information in two sources, you need to:

- identify all the relevant ideas and information in each source
- identify at least three points of comparison
- support each point in your comparison with short, relevant evidence from each source
- explain the significance of your chosen evidence in each source.

Now look at this exam-style question you saw at the start of the unit.

**Exam-style question**

You need to refer to **source A** and **source B** for this question.

Use details from **both** sources. Write a summary of the differences between the writers' experiences of going to bed.

(8 marks)

(1) Look at a paragraph written by one student in response to the exam-style question above.

| | | |
|---|---|---|
| identifies a key difference in the two sources | The writers describe two different experiences of going to bed in poor conditions. In source A, the writer describes how 'the tiles were off the roof and 'If it rained there was no shelter'. This makes you realise the bad conditions that people had to sleep in and there was nothing they could do about it. However, in source B, the writer describes how it was so cold that he had to put 'two pairs of woolen socks on your feet and another on your hands, and a hat with earflaps tied beneath the chin' and he soon warms up. This sounds much better than the experience described in source A because the writer could do something about the cold. | supports the key point with evidence from source A |
| supports the key point with evidence from source B | | explains the significance of the evidence |

(2) Can you identify all the elements the student has included in this paragraph? Link ✐ the annotations to the paragraph to show where the student has included them.

(3) Circle ⒶⒷ any adverbials that the student has used to signal comparison, for example:

| whereas | | but |
|---|---|---|

# Your turn!

You are now going to write your own answer in response to the exam-style question.

**Exam-style question**

You need to refer to **source A** and **source B** for this question.

Use details from **both** sources. Write a summary of the differences between the writers' experiences of going to bed. (8 marks)

**1** Complete 🖉 the planning table below.

|  | 1 | 2 | 3 |
|---|---|---|---|
| Note down **three key differences** you can write about in your response. |  |  |  |
| For each difference, choose a short, relevant **quotation** from each source. | Source A | Source A | Source A |
|  | Source B | Source B | Source B |
| Look at your chosen quotations. Note down any **explanation** that you feel they need. | Source A | Source A | Source A |
|  | Source B | Source B | Source B |

**2** Use your notes to write 🖉 your response to the exam-style question above on paper.

# Review your skills

## Check up

Review your response to the exam-style question on page 55. Tick ✓ the column to show how well you think you have done each of the following.

|  | Not quite ✓ | Nearly there ✓ | Got it! ✓ |
|---|---|---|---|
| identified key similarities | ☐ | ☐ | ☐ |
| supported points with relevant quotations from both sources | ☐ | ☐ | ☐ |
| explained the significance of evidence where needed | ☐ | ☐ | ☐ |

## Need more practice?

Here is another exam-style question, this time relating to source 2, *A letter from the Crimea* by Thomas Monks, on page 74, and source 3, an extract from *Going Commando* by Mark Time, on page 75. You'll find some suggested points to refer to in the Answers section.

### Exam-style question

You need to refer to **source 2** and **source 3** for this question.

Use details from both sources. Write a summary of the differences between the writers' experiences of life in the army.

(8 marks)

How confident do you feel about each of these **skills?** Colour ✏ in the bars.

**1** How do I identify points of comparison?

**2** How do I synthesise information and ideas in two sources?

**3** How do I write a comparison?

# ⑧ Comparing ideas and attitudes

This unit will help you compare the writers' ideas and attitudes in two different sources. The skills you will build are to:

• identify the writer's ideas and attitudes in each source

• explore ways to compare the two writers' ideas and attitudes

• structure an effective comparison.

In the exam, you will face questions like the one below. This is about the sources on page 58. This unit will prepare you to write your own response to this question.

**Exam-style question**

For this question, you need to refer to the **whole of source A**, together with **source B**.

Compare how the two writers convey their different attitudes to animals.

In your answer, you could:

• compare their different attitudes

• compare the methods they use to convey their attitudes

• support your ideas with references to both texts.

(16 marks)

Before you tackle the question you will work through three key questions in the **skills boosts** to help you compare the writers' ideas and attitudes.

 **How do I identify relevant ideas and attitudes?**

 **How do I compare ideas and attitudes?**

 **How do I develop my comparison?**

Read the two sources on page 58: an extract from *Never Cry Wolf* by Farley Mowat, published in 1963, and *A letter from Charles Darwin* written in 1838. You will tackle one 19th-century and one 20th- or 21st-century non-fiction extract in the Reading section of your Paper 2 exam.

## As you read, remember the following: ✓

| | | |
|---|---|---|
| Check you understand the focus of the exam question you are preparing to respond to. | Mark or highlight any ideas and information in each source that is relevant to the exam question. | Consider any similarities or differences in the writers' ideas and attitudes in each source. |

After several months observing a family of wolves in the Arctic Circle, naturalist Farley Mowat decided he needed to see the inside of their den (an underground burrow) while the wolves were out hunting.

**Source A** Never Cry Wolf, Farley Mowat

Reaching the entrance to the burrow I shed my heavy trousers, tunic and sweater, and taking a flashlight (whose batteries were very nearly dead) and measuring-tape from my pack, I began the difficult task of wiggling down the entrance tunnel.

The flashlight was so dim it cast only an orange glow – barely sufficient to enable me to read the marks on the
5 measuring-tape. I squirmed onward, descending at a forty-five-degree angle, for about eight feet. My mouth and eyes were soon full of sand and I was beginning to suffer from claustrophobia, for the tunnel was just big enough to admit me.

At the eight-foot mark the tunnel took a sharp upward bend and swung to the left. I pointed the torch in the new direction and pressed the switch. Four green lights in the murk ahead reflected back the dim torch beam.

10 In this case green was not my signal to advance. I froze where I was, while my startled brain tried to digest the information that at least two wolves were with me in the den.

Despite my close familiarity with the wolf family, this was the kind of situation where irrational but deeply ingrained prejudices completely overmaster reason and experience. To be honest, I was so frightened that paralysis gripped me. I had no weapon of any sort, and in my awkward posture I could barely have gotten one
15 hand free with which to ward off an attack. It seemed inevitable that the wolves would attack me, for even a gopher will make a fierce defense when he is cornered in his den.

The wolves did not even growl.

Save for the two faintly glowing pairs of eyes, they might not have been there at all.

In 1838, the naturalist Charles Darwin wrote a letter to his sister describing a visit to the Zoological Society in London – now known as London Zoo.

**Source B** A letter from Charles Darwin

Two days since, when it was very warm, I rode to the Zoological Society, and by the greatest piece of good fortune it was the first time this year, that the rhinoceros was turned out. Such a sight has seldom been seen, as to behold the rhinoceros kicking and rearing, (though neither end reached any great height) out of joy. It galloped up and down its court surprisingly quickly, like a huge cow, and it was marvellous how suddenly it could stop and turn
5 round at the end of each gallop. The elephant was in the adjoining yard and was greatly amazed at seeing the rhinoceros so frisk: he came close to the palings and after looking very intently, set off trotting himself, with his tail sticking out at one end and his trunk at the other, squealing and braying like half a dozen broken trumpets. I saw also the ourang-outang in great perfection: the keeper showed her an apple, but would not give it her, whereupon she threw herself on her back, kicked and cried, precisely like a naughty child. She then looked very
10 sulky and after two or three fits of passion, the keeper said, 'Jenny if you will stop bawling and be a good girl, I will give you the apple.' She certainly understood every word of this, and, though like a child, she had great work to stop whining, she at last succeeded, and then got the apple, with which she jumped into an arm chair and began eating it, with the most contented **countenance** imaginable.

countenance: face, expression

**How do I identify relevant ideas and attitudes?**

To begin identifying the writer's ideas and attitudes, you need to think about:
- the writer, what they are writing about and why
- the ideas in the source and what these suggest about the writer's attitudes and opinions.

(1) To identify the writer's attitudes, think about what the writer has written about and why. Read one student's notes below about source B on page 58, then look closely at source A and complete their notes.

|  | Source A | Source B |
|---|---|---|
| What is the source about? |  | A visit to the zoo |
| Who is the writer? | A naturalist studying wolves | A naturalist |
| Why are they writing it? |  | To describe how animals behave. |

(2) What do the ideas in the table suggest about the writer's ideas and attitudes? Complete the notes below.

Source A

| A. He wriggles into the wolves' burrow. | This shows the writer is very dedicated to learning more about wolves. |
|---|---|
| B. He sees the wolves and panics. | This suggests ............................................................................ |
| C. The wolves ignore him. | This gives the impression that ................................. |

Source B

| A. He describes the rhino galloping. | This suggests that he is amazed at how agile it is. |
|---|---|
| B. He describes the elephant's reaction. | ............................................................................................ |
| C. He describes the orang-utan behaving like a child. | ............................................................................................ |

(3) Write **one** sentence summarising **each** writer's ideas and attitudes about animals.

The writer of source A ............................................................................

................................................................................................................

The writer of source B ............................................................................

................................................................................................................

## 2 How do I compare ideas and attitudes?

When you compare sources, you need to look for ideas and attitudes that are:

- similar, or
- linked in some way but very different.

① Look at one student's notes on the writer's ideas and attitudes in source A on page 58.

> **Source A**
> A. The writer is very dedicated to learning more about wolves.
> B. Wolves are wild animals and can be very dangerous.
> C. Wolves may not behave how you expect them to – they may be more scared of you than you are of them.

Now think about the ideas and attitudes suggested in source B on page 58. Can you find a similarity or difference linked to the three key ideas in source A above?

**a** Does source B suggest that the writer is dedicated to learning more about the animals in the zoo? Tick ✓ **one** answer.

| Yes, this is a similarity. | ☐ | No, this is a difference. | ☐ |

Write ✐ **one** sentence explaining how source B is similar to or different from source A.

.......................................................................................................................................

.......................................................................................................................................

.......................................................................................................................................

**b** Does source B suggest that zoo animals can be wild or dangerous? Tick ✓ **one** answer.

| Yes, this is a similarity. | ☐ | No, this is a difference. | ☐ |

Write ✐ **one** sentence explaining why.

.......................................................................................................................................

.......................................................................................................................................

.......................................................................................................................................

**c** Does source B suggest that zoo animals behave unpredictably? Tick ✓ **one** answer.

| Yes, this is a similarity. | ☐ | No, this is a difference. | ☐ |

Write ✐ **one** sentence explaining why.

.......................................................................................................................................

.......................................................................................................................................

.......................................................................................................................................

# 3 How do I develop my comparison?

When you compare the writers' ideas and attitudes in two sources, you need to comment on **how** the writers use **language and structure** to express those ideas and attitudes.

1 Look at the sentences below, written by a student, comparing the writers' ideas and attitudes about animals in source A and source B on page 58.

> In both sources the writers suggest that animals can be unpredictable.

> For example, in source A, the writer bumps into two wolves in their den. He seems so sure that they will attack him, he is amazed that 'the wolves did not even growl'.

a Look at the quotation above from source A. The writer uses simple language and a short simple sentence to express this idea. Write ✎ **one or two** sentences explaining why the writer might have made these choices.

...................................................................................................................................................

...................................................................................................................................................

...................................................................................................................................................

b Now look at the start of the next sentence from the same student's response. Choose **one** quotation from source B on page 58 to support this point and add ✎ it to the response.

> The writer in source B also suggests that animals can be unpredictable because he seems surprised and amazed at the ways in which they behave:

...................................................................................................................................................

...................................................................................................................................................

...................................................................................................................................................

...................................................................................................................................................

...................................................................................................................................................

...................................................................................................................................................

...................................................................................................................................................

...................................................................................................................................................

...................................................................................................................................................

...................................................................................................................................................

c Look at your chosen quotation from source B above. Circle Ⓐ any words or phrases in the quotation which suggest that the writer is surprised and amazed at the animals' unpredictable behaviour.

d What do these words or phrases suggest about the writer and/or the animal's behaviour? Add ✎ **one or two** sentences to the response above, explaining your ideas.

# Comparing ideas and attitudes

To write a good comparison of the writers' ideas and attitudes in two sources, you need to:

- identify each writer's ideas and attitudes
- identify significant similarities or differences in the writers' ideas and attitudes
- support each similarity or difference you identify with evidence from each source
- comment on how each writer uses language and/or structure to express their ideas and attitudes.

Now look at the exam-style question you saw at the start of the unit.

**Exam-style question**

For this question, you need to refer to the **whole of source A**, together with **source B**.

Compare how the two writers convey their different attitudes to animals.

In your answer, you could:

- compare their different attitudes
- compare the methods they use to convey their attitudes
- support your ideas with references to both texts. **(16 marks)**

**(1)** Look at a paragraph written by one student in response to the exam-style question above.

| identifies a key similarity in the two sources |
| supports the key similarity with evidence from source A |
| explores the writer's use of language or structure in evidence from source A |

Both writers are fascinated by the animals they are writing about. The writer of source A goes to a lot of trouble to explore the wolves' den: 'I began the difficult task of wiggling down the entrance tunnel.' The word 'wiggling' shows how small and uncomfortable and difficult it was to get down there. Similarly, in source B, the writer shows how fascinated he is by describing the animal's behaviour in a lot of detail: 'Such a sight has seldom been seen, as to behold the rhinoceros kicking and rearing'. The phrase 'seldom been seen' suggests the writer thinks this is a surprising and amazing sight, which he is very excited about.

| compares the evidence from source A with evidence from source B |
| explores the writer's use of language or structure in evidence from source B |

**(2)** Can you identify all the elements the student has included in this paragraph? Link 🖉 the annotations to the paragraph to show where the student has included them.

**(3)** Circle Ⓐ any adverbials that the writer has used to signal comparison: for example,

| moreover | | also |

# Your turn!

You are now going to write your own answer in response to the exam-style question.

For this question, you need to refer to the **whole of source A**, together with **source B**.

Compare how the two writers convey their different attitudes to animals.

In your answer, you could:

- compare their different attitudes
- compare the methods they use to convey their attitudes
- support your ideas with references to both texts.

(16 marks)

(1) Complete ✎ the planning table below.

|  | 1 | 2 | 3 |
|---|---|---|---|
| Note down **three key similarities or differences** you can write about in your response. | | | |
| For each similarity or difference, choose a relevant **quotation** from each source. Circle any key words or phrases you could comment on. | Source A | Source A | Source A |
| | Source B | Source B | Source B |
| Look at each of your chosen quotations. Note down comments you could make about the writer's use of language and/or structure. | Source A | Source A | Source A |
| | Source B | Source B | Source B |

(2) Use your notes to write ✎ your response to the exam-style question above on paper.

# Review your skills

## Check up

Review your response to the exam-style question on page 63. Tick ✓ the column to show how well you think you have done each of the following.

| | Not quite ✓ | Nearly there ✓ | Got it ✓ |
|---|---|---|---|
| identified similarities and differences in the writers' ideas and attitudes | ☐ | ☐ | ☐ |
| supported my ideas with evidence from both sources | ☐ | ☐ | ☐ |
| developed my comparison with evidence from both sources | ☐ | ☐ | ☐ |

## Need more practice?

Below is another exam-style question, this time relating to source 2, *A letter from the Crimea* by Thomas Monks, on page 74, and source 3, an extract from *Going Commando* by Mark Time, on page 75. You'll find some suggested points to refer to in the Answers section.

### Exam-style question

For this question, you need to refer to the **whole of source 2**, together with **source 3**.

Compare how the two writers convey their different attitudes to life as a soldier.

In your answer, you could:

- compare their different attitudes
- compare the methods they use to convey their attitudes
- support your ideas with references to both texts.

(16 marks)

How confident do you feel about each of these **skills?** Colour ✏ in the bars.

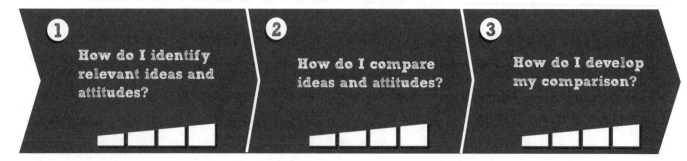

**1** How do I identify relevant ideas and attitudes?

**2** How do I compare ideas and attitudes?

**3** How do I develop my comparison?

# ⑨ Expressing your ideas clearly and precisely

This unit will help you express your ideas clearly and precisely. The skills you will build are to:

- use appropriately formal, analytical language to express your ideas
- select vocabulary to express your ideas precisely
- select sentence structures to express your ideas clearly.

In the exam, you will face questions like the one below. This is about the text on page 66. This unit will prepare you to write your own response to this question.

**Exam-style question**

You now need to refer **only** to **source A**, a text giving advice on bathing.

How does the writer use language to persuade the reader to take her advice?　　　　(12 marks)

The three key questions in the **skills boosts** will help you express your ideas clearly and precisely.

 **1** How do I write a formal, analytical response?

 **2** How do I express my ideas precisely?

 **3** How do I express my ideas clearly?

Read the extract on page 66 from *The Lady's Dressing Room* by Baroness Staffe, published in 1892. You will tackle a 19th-century non-fiction extract in the Reading section of your Paper 2 exam.

## As you read, remember the following:

Check you understand the focus of the exam question you are preparing to respond to.

Mark or highlight any parts of the text relevant to the question you are going to answer: where the writer tries to persuade the reader to take her advice.

In her book of advice for women, Baroness Staffe gives clear advice on taking a bath.

**Source A** The Lady's Dressing Room, Baroness Staffe

Regular bathing should enter into the habits of all classes of society. If it is absolutely impossible to immerse oneself completely every day in a large bath, or if it is forbidden by the doctor, a sponge-bath may be considered sufficient for the needs of cleanliness and health.

5 The human skin is a complicated network, whose meshes it is necessary to keep free and open. The healthy action of the pores of the skin is stimulated by the bath, especially if it is followed by friction with a rough towel. Both fevers and contagious **maladies** of many kinds are often avoided by such simple precautions as these.

In cases of internal inflammation and congestion, and of bilious colic, there is no more certain remedy than a hot bath. It is also known to have worked surprising cures in cases of obstinate constipation. Anyone who is afraid of having caught a contagious malady should immediately have recourse to a hot bath, as it is quite possible that
10 the infection may make its way out of the body through the pores. Of course, particular care would be needed not to take a chill on leaving the bath.

Cleanliness of the skin has a great effect in the proper **assimilation** of nourishment by the body; and it has even been recognised that well-washed pigs yield superior meat to those that are allowed to indulge their **propensities** for wallowing in the mire.

15 There are many people who immerse themselves every day for a few instants in a cold bath; one must be very strong to support this form of bath, and it is perhaps wiser not to try it without having consulted a doctor. Even when the cold bath is allowed, it is best to take only one plunge and come out at once. The water ought to be about **50° to 60° Fahrenheit**.

The hot bath is good for those who are subject to a rush of blood to the head. Its temperature should not
20 exceed **100°**.

The tepid bath is the one most used, and its temperature may range from 68° to 96°. It is a mistake to remain too long in a tepid bath; thirty minutes is the maximum time one should stay therein, and it is perhaps best to leave it after a quarter of an hour, unless of course medical orders decide otherwise.

If it is impossible, for various reasons, to have a large bath every day, a sponge bath will replace it conveniently,
25 and is sufficient for the necessities of health and cleanliness. One should begin by taking a sponge bath of tepid water, and then by degrees one can lower the temperature of the water until at last the daily tub is a cold one. In all cases, however, the bath-room should be slightly warmed in winter, spring, and autumn; and care should be taken that the towels are warm and dry. It is often a good thing to take a little air and exercise after the bath, but only on condition of walking very fast. Never take a bath, or in any way immerse yourself in water, immediately
30 after having eaten; a bath would be distinctly dangerous, and even minor **ablutions** are apt to trouble the digestion. One should allow three hours to elapse between any meal at all copious and a bath.

maladies: illnesses
assimilation: absorbing, taking into the body
propensities: habits
50° to 60° Fahrenheit: approximately 10–15° Celsius
100°: approximately 38° Celsius
ablutions: washing yourself

# How do I write a formal, analytical response?

The most successful responses are written in a formal, analytical style.

(1) Look at the opening of one student's response, commenting on how the writer uses language in the extract on page 66 to persuade the reader to take her advice.

> The writer explains that: 'fevers and contagious maladies of many kinds are often avoided' by taking a bath and drying yourself with a rough towel.

Look at all the words and phrases below which you could use to add to the above response.

**A.**

- [ ] i. This makes me think that
- [ ] ii. This means that
- [ ] iii. This suggests that
- [ ] iv. This creates the impression that
- [ ] v. This implies that
- [ ] vi. This indicates that
- [ ] vii. This tells me that

bathing is

**B.**

- i. a necessity [ ]
- ii. a must [ ]
- iii. a no brainer [ ]
- iv. essential [ ]
- v. important [ ]
- vi. a big deal [ ]
- vii. vital [ ]

**a** Which of the words and phrases above would you **not** use because they are **too informal**? Cross ⊗ them.

**b** Which of the words and phrases **might** you use because they are appropriate for a formal, analytical piece of writing? Tick ✓ them.

**c** Which of the words and phrases would **you** add to the above response? Choose **one** from column A and one from column B and circle Ⓐ them.

(2) Look at another comment from the student's response.

> The writer says that for 'internal inflammation and congestion... there is no more certain remedy than a hot bath'. The phrase 'no more certain' makes it sound like a bath is definitely going to sort your illness out and nothing else will do the job.

**a** Circle Ⓐ all the words and phrases that you feel could be more formal and/or analytical.

**b** Rewrite ✎ the comment, making it as formal and analytical as possible.

.......................................................................................................................

.......................................................................................................................

.......................................................................................................................

## 2  How do I express my ideas precisely?

When you write about a text, choose your vocabulary carefully to express your ideas as precisely as possible.

① Look at a paragraph from one student's response, commenting on how the writer persuades the reader to take her advice in the extract on page 66.

Choose one word to fill ✎ each gap. Choose the word that you feel:

- describes the writer's ideas most accurately

- expresses how the writer uses language most precisely.

| says |
| --- |
| explains |
| advises |
| warns |
| suggests |

The writer ......................... that 'Anyone who is afraid of having caught a contagious malady should immediately have recourse to a hot bath'. The words 'afraid' and 'immediately' imply that you should be ......................... and follow the writer's advice ......................... .

| worried |
| --- |
| scared |
| concerned |
| anxious |
| terrified |

| soon |
| --- |
| straight away |
| urgently |
| instantly |
| quickly |

② Now look at this comment about how the writer persuades the reader to take her advice.

A.        B.        C.

Throughout the article, the writer seems sure that her facts are good and her advice is good.

**a** Note down ✎ two words which could be used to replace each of the highlighted words and express these ideas more precisely.

A. .................................... ☐ ........................................ ☐

B. .................................... ☐ ........................................ ☐

C. .................................... ☐ ........................................ ☐

**b** Which of the words that you noted would you choose to use in the comment above? Tick ✓ them.

# 3 How do I express my ideas clearly?

Short sentences can be used to express ideas simply. Linking **two or three** of those ideas **clearly and carefully** in a longer sentence can show how those ideas are related.

① Look at two students' ideas below, expressed in short sentences.

Rewrite ✎ their ideas, giving **two different versions** of each group of sentences, linking them to form a longer single sentence. In each version, experiment with:

- using different conjunctions (see word box for ideas) to link the ideas

**and/or**

- re-ordering the two or three ideas in the sentence.

| Conjunctions | |
|---|---|
| when | although |
| | and |
| because | but |
| however | as |

**a** The writer suggests that you can prevent illness with a hot bath. Your skin is a 'complicated network'. It opens the pores of your skin.

Version 1 ....................................................................................................

....................................................................................................  ☐

Version 2 ....................................................................................................

....................................................................................................  ☐

**b** The writer advises that you should never take a bath immediately after eating. It could be dangerous. You can if you 'allow three hours to elapse'.

Version 1 ....................................................................................................

....................................................................................................  ☐

Version 2 ....................................................................................................

....................................................................................................  ☐

**c** Look at each pair of sentences you have written. Which one of each pair is most clearly expressed? Tick ✓ it.

② Look at another student's notes on the extract on page 66.

| | |
|---|---|
| the proper assimilation of nourishment | baths help you digest food properly |
| well-washed pigs yield superior meat | clean pigs produce better-quality meat |
| wallowing in the mire | suggests people who don't bathe are like pigs |

Use the notes to write ✎ **one or two** sentences in which all of the student's ideas are carefully linked using conjunctions.

....................................................................................................

....................................................................................................

....................................................................................................

# Expressing your ideas clearly and precisely

To express your ideas clearly and precisely, you need to:

- express your ideas in a formal analytical style
- choose your vocabulary carefully to ensure you are expressing your ideas precisely
- use some shorter sentences to express your ideas clearly and simply
- use some longer sentences, linking ideas using carefully chosen conjunctions.

Now look at the exam-style question you saw at the start of the unit.

## Exam-style question

You now need to refer **only** to **source A**, a text giving advice on bathing.

How does the writer use language to persuade the reader to take her advice?          (12 marks)

(1) Look at this paragraph from one student's response to the task.

> The writer gives the reader some pretty serious warnings about when to have a bath. She says, 'Never take a bath, or in any way immerse yourself in water, immediately after having eaten; a bath would be distinctly dangerous'. The words 'never' and 'in any way' make it sound like this is really important and the word 'dangerous' sounds like she's trying to scare the reader but she doesn't say why it is dangerous and you get the idea that you really must do what she says.

a Is this paragraph written in a formal, analytical style? Circle (A) any words or phrases you feel could be improved. Note (✎) your suggested improvements in the margin.

b Could any of the vocabulary choices in the paragraph above be made more precise? Underline (A) any words or phrases you feel could be improved. Note (✎) your suggested improvements in the margin.

c One sentence in this paragraph is very long. How could you break it down into shorter sentences? How could you use a wider range of conjunctions to link some of the ideas and express them more clearly? Rewrite (✎) the sentence below.

.................................................................................................................................

.................................................................................................................................

.................................................................................................................................

.................................................................................................................................

.................................................................................................................................

.................................................................................................................................

# Your turn!

You are now going to write your own answer in response to the exam-style question.

> **Exam-style question**
>
> You now need to refer **only** to **source A**, a text giving advice on bathing.
>
> How does the writer use language to persuade the reader to take her advice    **(12 marks)**

In your exam, you should spend around **15 minutes** on this type of question and write **two or three** paragraphs. However, you are now going to write just **one** paragraph. This will allow you to focus more closely on expressing your ideas as clearly and precisely as possible.

**1** Look at some of the ways the writer tries to persuade the reader to take her advice.

| | | |
|---|---|---|
| **Advantages** | The healthy action of the pores of the skin is stimulated by the bath, especially if it is followed by friction with a rough towel. | ☐ |
| | Anyone who is afraid of having caught a contagious malady should immediately have recourse to a hot bath | ☐ |
| **Warnings** | It is a mistake to remain too long in a tepid bath | ☐ |
| | Never take a bath, or in any way immerse yourself in water, immediately after having eaten | ☐ |
| **Helpful tips** | Even when the cold bath is allowed, it is best to take only one plunge and come out at once. The water ought to be about 50° to 60° Fahrenheit. | ☐ |
| | the bath-room should be slightly warmed in winter, spring, and autumn; and care should be taken that the towels are warm and dry. | ☐ |

**a** Choose **one** of the above which you can explore in your response to the exam-style question. Tick ✓ it.

**b** Use it to write ✎ a paragraph in response to the exam-style question. Remember to:

- write in a formal, analytical style
- choose your vocabulary carefully to express your ideas precisely
- think about how you structure your sentence to express your ideas clearly.

..................................................................................................................................

..................................................................................................................................

..................................................................................................................................

..................................................................................................................................

..................................................................................................................................

..................................................................................................................................

# Review your skills

## Check up

Review your response to the exam-style question on page 71. Tick ✓ the column to show how well you think you have done each of the following.

| | Not quite ✓ | Nearly there ✓ | Got it! ✓ |
|---|---|---|---|
| written in a formal, analytical style | ☐ | ☐ | ☐ |
| chosen vocabulary to express my ideas precisely | ☐ | ☐ | ☐ |
| chosen sentence structures to express my ideas clearly | ☐ | ☐ | ☐ |

## Need more practice?

You can EITHER:

(1) Look again at your paragraph written in response to the exam-style question on page 71. Rewrite it, experimenting with different vocabulary choices and sentence structures, linking your ideas in different ways. Which are most effective in expressing your ideas clearly and precisely?

AND/OR

(2) Choose a **second** piece of advice from the suggestions on page 71. Write a further paragraph in response to the exam-style question, focusing closely on your vocabulary choice and sentence structures.

How confident do you feel about each of these **skills?** Colour in the bars.

**1** How do I write a formal, analytical response?

**2** How do I express my ideas precisely?

**3** How do I express my ideas clearly?

# More practice texts

This is the opening of a short story.

The judge of the United States court of the district lying along the Rio Grande border found the following letter one morning in his mail:

JUDGE:

When you sent me up for four years you made a talk. Among other hard things, you called me a

5      rattlesnake. Maybe I am one -- anyhow, you hear me rattling now. One year after I got to the pen, my daughter died of -- well, they said it was poverty and the disgrace together. You've got a daughter, Judge, and I'm going to make you know how it feels to lose one. And I'm going to bite that district attorney that spoke against me. I'm free now, and I guess I've turned to rattlesnake all right. I feel like one. I don't say much, but this is my rattle. Look out when I strike.

10      Yours respectfully,

RATTLESNAKE.

Judge Derwent threw the letter carelessly aside. It was nothing new to receive such epistles from desperate men whom he had been called upon to judge. He felt no alarm. Later on he showed the letter to Littlefield, the young district attorney, for Littlefield's name was included in the threat, and the judge was **punctilious** in matters

15 between himself and his fellow men.

Littlefield honoured the rattle of the writer, as far as it concerned himself, with a smile of contempt; but he frowned a little over the reference to the Judge's daughter, for he and Nancy Derwent were to be married in the fall.

Littlefield went to the clerk of the court and looked over the records with him. They decided that the letter might

20 have been sent by Mexico Sam, a half-breed border desperado who had been imprisoned for manslaughter four years before. Then official duties crowded the matter from his mind, and the rattle of the revengeful serpent was forgotten.

Court was in session at Brownsville. Most of the cases to be tried were charges of smuggling, counterfeiting, post-office robberies, and violations of Federal laws along the border. One case was that of a young Mexican, Rafael

25 Ortiz, who had been rounded up by a clever deputy marshal in the act of passing a counterfeit silver dollar. He had been suspected of many such **deviations from rectitude**, but this was the first time that anything provable had been fixed upon him. Ortiz languished cozily in jail, smoking brown cigarettes and waiting for trial. Kilpatrick, the deputy, brought the counterfeit dollar and handed it to the district attorney in his office in the court-house. The deputy and a reputable **druggist** were prepared to swear that Ortiz paid for a bottle of medicine with it. The coin

30 was a poor counterfeit, soft, dull-looking, and made principally of lead. It was the day before the morning on which the docket would reach the case of Ortiz, and the district attorney was preparing himself for trial.

"Not much need of having in high-priced experts to prove the coin's queer, is there, Kil?"smiled Littlefield, as he thumped the dollar down upon the table, where it fell with no more ring than would have come from a lump of putty.

**punctilious:** showing great attention to detail
**deviations from rectitude:** wrong-doings, crimes
**druggist:** chemist, pharmacist

This letter was written by a soldier during the Crimean War (1853–6).

**Source 2** A letter from the Crimea, Thomas Monks, 1854

My dear Father

I now take the opportunity of writing to you, hoping to find you all well, as this leaves me quite well, thank God for it. I suppose you have been anxious about me because I did not write to you before, but the reason was, because I could not get any paper to write on.

5 I suppose you have heard about the battle we had on the 25th of October. If you could see *The Times* of November the 12th, you will see a very good account of our regiment, and the old Scotch Greys, who made a grand charge against double their number. The heavy brigade got great credit for that day; but I am sorry to say the light brigade got cut up. They lost about 600 out of 800. It made me feel very much when we went out to cover them, to see them fall. It brought us under a very heavy cross fire from the enemy, the **balls** and shells bursting beside us.
10 A ball would burst under a horse, and blow it to pieces, and never hurt the man. You would see men running back with their arms off, and others bleeding from all parts of their bodies.

I can tell you, dear father, when one thinks about home, it is enough to make one cry; but I will hope we will have sunny days for these yet. It is now December, and we are in camp yet. We had a great storm about a week ago. I was on trumpeter's guard at the time the storm came across the plain, accompanied by hailstones and snow, and
15 it blew all our tents down. The only way to keep still was to lie down. I had to do so for fear of being borne among the dirt. You may think in what sort of state our tents were, as after it was all over, we had to lay down that night on the wet ground without anything to eat, the cooks being unable to keep the fires in. Ever since then it has been very wet and cold. Our poor horses are dying by sections every day, and **Sebastopol** is not taken yet, though we have had about seven weeks' hard fighting at it. I was on **picket** the other day; we have to stay out all night with
20 our horses, and it was very wet and cold. I don't think we can stand this much longer, but still we all keep up our spirits well. I can only hope we may get one more good charge at them and finish it. I must now conclude for the present, and I hope I have eased your mind about me. Accept of my kind love yourself, and no more from your affectionate son,

Thomas Monks, trumpeter, 6th Enniskillen Dragoons.

25 P.S. The guns are firing away now. We are about two miles off them, but we can see the flash and smoke. You may guess what sort of state we are in when I tell you I have not had a chance of washing my face these four weeks, let alone having a clean shirt. We are, I am sorry to say, in a state of filth, but we do the best we can.

balls: cannon balls
Sebastopol: a town in the Crimea, eventually captured from the Russians in September 1855
picket: on duty, looking out for the enemy

At the age of 16, Mark Time decided he wanted to become a Royal Marine Commando. In this extract, he begins his basic training.

**Source 3** Going Commando, Mark Time, 2015

Despite it being near-freezing, the PTI wore only a snow-white vest on his top half. 'Keep moving, fellas,' he yelled, before barking out instructions at high speed. 'No one stands still on the bottom field! Five-second sprint GO! Ten press-ups, ten sit-ups, ten star-jumps, GO! Roll over, roll over, roll over, ten sit-ups, GO! Roll over, roll over, roll over that wall, GO! Back again, not quick enough! Front support position place! That's press-ups to you, fellas. Arms
5   bend and stretch arms, bend and stretch. Ten star-jumps, GO! Hurry up! Not quick enough, that wall, GO!'

And so it continued, a white noise of incomprehensible, ungrammatical shouting that confused us to the point of doing everything wrong. Some of us were doing press-ups while others were rolling into those who were still doing sit-ups, or tripping up people who were sprinting like headless chickens in no discernible direction.

Knackered by the warm-up, we moved on to the height confidence test. Before us stood a large steel structure
10   with thin wooden planks spanning its length. Not ever having been higher than the climbing frame at primary school, I really didn't know how I'd cope at 7m up. As I stood at the bottom of the ladder ready to climb, I hoped my legs didn't turn to jelly like the lad in front of me.

'Come on you, don't take all day,' shouted the PTI – I hoped at someone else.

'I can't do it, Corporal,' the guy above me shouted.

15   'Can't or won't?' the PTI shouted back.

I don't think he was in a position to respond to such a rhetorical question. He just stood transfixed on the ladder, his knuckles white from his vice-like grip.

'Right, get down. Hurry up!'

The lad slowly made his way down the ladder. He was sent over to the PRC corporal and sat down. I doubted he
20   would become a Royal Marine – or a window cleaner, for that matter.

It did nothing for my own confidence, but once I was up there I felt okay, despite having only a narrow plank of bendy wood between me and **quadriplegia**.

Although I'd thought myself pretty fit – playing sport almost continuously and being able to outrun the police – I'd never felt the pain of cramp. Running up the hill towards the metal gate on the assault course, I felt it for
25   the first time. I managed to finish, wincing with pain, and veered towards a PTI who laughingly pulled me to the floor. He stretched my calves to ease the pain and sent me on my way to warm down. I thought I'd blown my chance. Needing immediate attention after completing the assault course surely meant I wasn't fit enough to pass?

quadriplegia: paralysis of the arms and legs, caused by injury or illness

# Answers

## Unit 1

### Page 3

① KEY: E; DETAIL: A, B, C; X: D

② ⓐ For example:

Paragraphs 2 and 3: Something is wrong. The cows are not behaving normally.

Paragraph 4: Something is wrong. A soldier shouts at them.

Paragraphs 5–7: Janet ignores the soldier, walks on and collapses.

Paragraphs 8–10: Richard hurries towards her and collapses.

### Page 4

① **narrate** (for example, recounting events, the narrator's thoughts, etc., throughout the extract); **describe** (for example, the landscape, the village in the distance, etc.)

② ⓐ ⓑ

A. The soldier, the sleeping cows, the characters collapsing, all suggest strange and disturbing events and create a sense of mystery.
B. Collapsing humans and cows, and the presence of the military, all suggest danger.
C. The narrator and his wife have collapsed but it is not clear why.

### Page 5

① ⓐ D is the most relevant and accurate summary of the extract.

ⓑ For example, combining some elements of the summaries and adding further key information: Something very strange is happening in the village of Midwich and people are in danger.

② At the start of the text, everything seems perfectly normal. By the end of the text, we are left with the very clear impression that something strange and very dangerous is happening.

### Page 6

① 1–3 are correct.

② 4 is incorrect. There is no evidence to support this assumption. Correct answers could include, for example: he wants Richard and Janet to turn back; his shouting is 'unintelligible'; he shouts more loudly when he is ignored; etc.

### Page 7

For example:

- It is in the countryside.
- It is surrounded by fields and trees.
- There are farms near to the village.
- It has a church.

### Page 8

- He was sent to prison for four years.
- His daughter died.
- He is going to take his revenge on the judge and the district attorney.
- He has been released from prison.

## Unit 2

### Page 11

① ⓑ All are arguable.

### Page 12

① ⓐ For example: 'the ground seemed to be covered with little illumination lamps, such as are hung on Christmas-trees.'

### Page 13

① A: More effective
B: Most effective
C: Least effective

② For example:

The writer describes looking down on London, saying it looks like 'a mere rubbish heap'. This suggests the writer's low opinion of the city. He sees it as dirty and smelly, small and unimportant. The word 'mere' makes it sound even less important.

### Page 14

①

| identifies a relevant idea from the text | The writer describes how polluted London is |
| --- | --- |
| supports it with a quotation from the text | 'the dense fumes from the million chimneys' |
| comments on the effect of the writer's choices | shows how much smoke there would be and how it covered the whole of London |
| comments on the impact of the writer's choices on the reader | helps you imagine how thick and choking they would be… It makes the whole city sound disgusting and dirty. |

② For example:

The writer describes how polluted London is: 'the dense fumes from the million chimneys'. This shows how polluted London is. The writer says the fumes are 'dense' which helps you imagine how thick and choking they would be, especially when he says 'the million chimneys' which shows how much smoke there would be and how it covered the whole of London. It makes the whole city sound disgusting and dirty.

## Page 16

### Words, phrases and language features

- Monks describes the life of a soldier as 'enough to make one cry', suggesting he feels upset and frightened.
- Repetition of 'wet and cold' emphasises the difficult conditions in which he is living.
- The phrase 'state of filth' again suggests difficult conditions.

### Sentence forms

- Longer sentence contrasts difficult conditions and positive attitude: 'I don't think we can stand this much longer, but still we all keep up our spirits well.'
- A short dramatic sentence announces the beginning of fighting: 'The guns are firing away now.'

# Unit 3

## Page 19

**1** **a** H is not featured in the extract.

**b** A, B and C are the focus of the extract.

## Page 20

**1** **a** Both are arguable. 'Likes expensive things' is, perhaps, more apparent in this section of the text.

**b c d** For example: 'his oxidized gold cigarette case' and 'best quality folio typing paper' suggest Fleming's expensive tastes.

**2** For example: 'rattled the story down'; 'swift assurance'; '2,000 words a day'

## Page 21

**1** **a** All are arguable, although the suggestion that 'Bond is a baby' would need further explanation!

**b** All are arguable.

**2** For example: 'rattled' suggests the sound of the typewriter and the pace at which Fleming wrote the novel, adding to the impression that he wrote the novel 'effortlessly'.

## Page 22

| uses key words from the question | One way the writer interests the reader |
| --- | --- |
| identifies a key idea in the text | is by showing what Ian Fleming was like. |
| explains the impression created | The writer creates the impression that Fleming had a strict routine when he wrote his stories. |
| identifies a word or phrase that creates that impression | The writer explains that Fleming would write his story 'Every morning between nine and twelve'. The phrase 'every morning' |
| comments on what the word or phrase suggests | suggests he did the same thing every day |
| comments on what the word or phrase makes the reader think or feel | which makes me think he was a very organised and determined person. |

## Page 24

### Words, phrases and language features

- Vivid description of the other trainee's fear: 'transfixed on the ladder, his knuckles white from his vice-like grip'
- Description of the structure the writer has to climb suggests his fear: 'a narrow plank of bendy wood between me and quadriplegia'
- 'wincing with pain' suggests the training is very demanding

### Sentence forms

- PTI speaks in short exclamations to suggest he is barking demanding instructions: 'Right, get down. Hurry up!'
- Rhetorical question at the end of the extract suggests the writer's anxiety.

# Unit 4

## Page 27

**1** **a** For example:
- A: I pulled too hard.
- B: Instantly, it began to deflate.
- C: That, combined with the eddies swirling from the trees and buildings ahead, caused a break in the airflow under the canopy.
- D: That, combined with the eddies swirling from the trees and buildings ahead, caused a break in the airflow under the canopy. Instantly, it began to deflate.

**b** For example: The first, longer sentence form includes a long list of all the negative feelings the writer experienced as he fell, suggesting how long he had to experience them all. The second, shorter sentence form suggests his increasing speed. The final, very short sentence form makes the ending seem all the more dramatic and sudden.

## Page 28

**1** **a** All are valid.

**b** All are valid.

**2** This short, blunt sentence dramatically emphasises the writer suddenly realising what is happening, particularly in contrast to the longer sentence before it. It helps to create a feeling of shock and fear.

## Page 29

**1** i. B
ii. A
iii. C

**2** **3** All are valid choices.

## Page 30

| | |
|---|---|
| uses key words from the question | The writer makes the reader understand how he felt |
| identifies a significant impression created in the text | by building up the tension as he describes falling to the ground: |
| identifies a significant sentence form | Using short sentences |
| comments on how that sentence form adds to the impression created | makes it sound like it is happening very quickly and like he is panicking… the short sentence makes you realise how everything stopped when he hit it. |
| identifies a significant choice of word or phrase | The last one of these short sentences is just one word 'Wallop'. |
| comments on how that word or phrase adds to the impression created | This word makes you realise how hard he hit the ground |

## Page 32

### Words, phrases and language features

- Referring to himself as 'Rattlesnake' suggests he is still angry that the judge called him this – and that he wants to frighten the judge.
- 'Maybe I am one' suggests he may accept he has done wrong.
- The words 'bite' and 'strike' suggest the actions of an angry snake.

### Sentence forms

- Short sentences throughout suggest his anger.
- The dash in 'my daughter died of -- well, they said it was poverty' creates a pause, suggesting he is hesitating to say how his daughter died, implying his shame and upset.

# Unit 5

## Page 35

1. a. Harold Fry

   b. Harold and Maureen

   c. Harold gets a letter. This event dominates the opening and 'would change everything', we are told in the opening sentence.

## Page 36

1. i. E
   ii. C
   iii. C, R
   iv. S
   v. E
   vi. E

2. Arguably, the more significant quotations are:
   i. The importance of the letter is emphasised at the very start.
   ii. This suggests that Harold's life is uneventful and he feels trapped.
   iii. This suggests that their relationship has deteriorated.
   v. The fact that the letter is from a hospice suggests that Queenie is terminally ill.

## Page 37

1. a b All are valid.
2. For example: The words 'would change everything' tell you how important this letter is going to be in Harold's life. It engages the reader immediately to make them want to find out what the letter is about, who it is from, and the impact it will have.

## Page 38

| | |
|---|---|
| uses key words from the question | The writer has structured the text |
| identifies a feature of the text's structure | to focus the reader's attention on the letter from the beginning |
| comments on what the writer has done in that feature | makes it sound very mysterious |
| comments on how the writer has that feature's effect | This makes me think Harold and Maureen never get letters so this must be something special or strange. It's also pink and Harold doesn't recognise the writing on it so it suggests that the letter inside will be something exciting and unexpected. |
| comments on its impact on the reader | You really want to find out who the letter is from and why they are writing to Harold and how it will change everything. |

## Page 40

- The writer immediately engages the reader with a threatening letter.
- Rattlesnake's anger contrasts with the judge's calm reaction: 'He felt no alarm.'
- The story of Rattlesnake is soon replaced by the story of the counterfeiter, encouraging the reader to read on to find out if there is a connection between them, and whether the counterfeiter will be found guilty.

# Unit 6

## Page 43

1. All are valid.
2. A, B, C
3. For example: The writer makes you wonder what has happened using the narrator considering different possibilities. The ending is a surprise because it is none of these possibilities and the problem is still a threat to both Harry and the narrator.

## Page 44

1. 'Sshhh!', whispered, For God's sake don't make a noise, Please
2. Top two comments – X

   Other comments on the left – W

   Other comments on the right – H

**3** **a** 'Don't touch the bed! For God's sake don't touch the bed!'... shot in the stomach

**b** The repetitive exclamations and the narrator's description of Pope's voice suggest his fear and panic.

## Page 45

**1** **a** All are valid.

## Page 46

| identifies where the writer has tried to achieve their intention | Just before you find out what has actually happened, the narrator describes Harry Pope: 'He was lying there very still and tense as though he was holding on to himself hard because of sharp pain.' |
|---|---|
| comments on what the writer has done | The writer makes you think he has been bitten by the snake and is dying in agony |
| comments on how what the writer has done helps the writer's intention | by describing how hard he is holding himself and the pain as sharp |
| comments on the success of its impact on the reader | This is very dramatic but the story becomes really tense when you find out the snake is still there and could bite him at any minute. |

## Page 48

- The letter is attention-grabbing because it threatens violence and revenge.
- The writer makes you feel sympathy for Rattlesnake by including details of his daughter's death.
- The writer makes you dislike the judge and the district attorney. He describes how the judge is not alarmed by the letter and the attorney smiles with 'contempt', suggesting neither has any sympathy with Rattlesnake.

# Unit 7

## Page 51

**1** **a** Source A: All are relevant.

Source B: A, B and C are not relevant.

**b** For example:

E. The bedding is not washed very often.

F. The beds are infested with vermin.

G. None of the people who sleep there have to wash.

All are relevant.

**c** For example:

F. The writer puts on layers and layers of clothing to try to keep warm.

G. The writer then has lots and lots of blankets, coats and a carpet put on him. It's like 'sleeping under a dead horse'.

H. At first it is freezing but he soon warms up.

All are relevant.

## Page 52

**1** For example:

A. roof

B. other people

C. payment

D. discomfort

E. dirt

**2** For example:

In source A, the writer focuses on the dirty conditions in which he has to sleep whereas in source B the writer focuses on how cold it is and what he has to do to keep warm.

## Page 53

**1** **a** For example:

Source A: 'Dirt is the rule with them, and cleanliness the exception. They are all infested with vermin.'

Source B: 'First, you put on long underwear, pajamas, jeans, a sweatshirt, your grandfather's old cardigan and bathrobe, two pairs of woolen socks on your feet and another on your hands, and a hat with earflaps tied beneath the chin.'

**b** For example:

In source A, the writer describes how 'dirt is the rule with them' and 'They are all infested with vermin'.

However, the writer of source B describes how he had to put on 'long underwear, pajamas, jeans' and 'two pairs of woolen socks on your feet and another on your hands'.

**c** This gives the impression that lodging houses were disgusting places to sleep.

This suggests how very cold it was sleeping in the porch.

## Page 54

**1**

| identifies a key difference in the two sources | The writers describe two different experiences of going to bed in poor conditions. |
|---|---|
| supports the key point with evidence from source A | In source A, the writer describes how 'the tiles were off the roof' and 'If it rained there was no shelter'. |
| supports the key point with evidence from source B | However, in source B, the writer describes how it was so cold that he had to put 'two pairs of woolen socks on your feet and another on your hands, and a hat with earflaps tied beneath the chin' and he soon warms up. |
| explains the significance of the evidence | This makes you realise the bad conditions that people had to sleep in and there was nothing they could do about it.... This sounds much better than the experience described in source A because the writer could do something about the cold. |

**2**  However

## Page 56

- Source 2 focuses on war; source 3 focuses on training.
- Source 2 describes the horrors of battle; there is no mention of combat in source 3.
- Source 2 focuses on the filth in which the soldiers live in a battle situation; source 3 focuses on the ordeal of completing physical challenges.

# Unit 8

## Page 59

**(1)** What is the source about? Exploring a wolves' den.

Why are they writing it? It is a surprising story about how wolves behave.

**(2)** **Source A**

B. This suggests he is in a very dangerous situation.

C. This gives the impression that wolves are not as dangerous as we might think.

**Source B**

B. This suggests he finds the elephant amusing and entertaining.

C. This suggests that the writer thinks animals and humans are more similar than we might think.

**(3)** The writer of source A cannot help being frightened when he is trapped with wolves, but they seem to be even more frightened of him.

The writer of source B finds animals amusing, entertaining and surprisingly like humans.

## Page 60

**(1)** **(a)** No; the writer seems to be observing the animals' entertaining behaviour, not finding out more about them.

**(b)** No; although the writer describes their unpredictable behaviour, there is no suggestion that they are dangerous.

**(b)** Yes, the writer seems surprised at their unpredictable behaviour: the rhino's wild galloping and the orang-utan behaving like a child.

## Page 61

**(1)** **(a)** The simple language and short, simple sentence structure add emphasis to this point, highlighting the writer's surprise.

**(b)** For example: 'it was marvellous how suddenly it could stop and turn round at the end of each gallop'

**(c)** **(d)** The word 'marvellous' suggests the writer's amazement and how enthusiastic he feels at the sight of the rhino galloping.

## Page 62

**(1)**

| identifies a key similarity in the two sources | Both writers are fascinated by the animals they are writing about. |
|---|---|
| supports the key similarity with evidence from source A | The writer of source A goes to a lot of trouble to explore the wolves' den: 'I began the difficult task of wiggling down the entrance tunnel.' |
| explores the writer's use of language or structure in evidence from source A | The word 'wiggling' shows how small and uncomfortable and difficult it was to get down there. |
| compares the evidence from source A with evidence from source B | Similarly, in source B, the writer shows how fascinated he is by describing the animal's behaviour in a lot of detail: 'Such a sight has seldom been seen, as to behold the rhinoceros kicking and rearing'. |
| explores the writer's use of language or structure in evidence from source B | The phrase 'seldom been seen' suggests the writer thinks this is a surprising and amazing sight, which he is very excited about. |

**(2)** Both, Similarly

## Page 64

- Both texts show the difficulties of life as a soldier. source 2 suggests the pain of being away from home: 'it is enough to make one cry'; source 3 vividly describes the pain of completing an assault course: 'wincing with pain'.
- Source 3 clearly shows the role of senior officers and their relationship with the soldiers: "Ten star-jumps, GO! Hurry up! Not quick enough, that wall, GO!"; in source 2 there is no mention of officers.
- Source 2 is surprisingly positive: 'We are, I am sorry to say, in a state of filth, but we do the best we can.'; source 3 expects failure: 'Needing immediate attention after completing the assault course surely meant I wasn't fit enough to pass?'

# Unit 9

## Page 67

**(1)** **(a)** In column A, all are appropriately formal. In column B, ii, iii, and vi are inappropriately informal.

**(b)** In column A, iii, iv, v, vi and vii are more appropriate for a formal analytical response. In column B, i, iv, v and vii are more appropriate for a formal analytical response.

**(2)** **(a)** For example: says, makes it sound like, sort ... out, do the job

**(b)** For example: The writer ~~says~~ explains that for 'internal inflammation and congestion... there is no more certain remedy than a hot bath.' The phrase 'no more certain' ~~makes it sound like~~ suggests that a bath is definitely going to ~~sort your illness out~~ cure the illness and nothing else will ~~do the job~~ work as effectively.

## Page 68

**1** All are acceptable; however, the most precise, accurate choices are arguably:

- advises, suggests
- concerned, anxious
- urgently, instantly.

**2** **a** For example:

A. certain, convinced, confident

B. correct, accurate, true

C. appropriate, sound, effective, wise

## Page 69

**1** **a** For example:

- The writer suggests that you can prevent illness with a hot bath <u>because</u> your skin is a 'complicated network' <u>and</u> it opens the pores of your skin.
- <u>Because</u> your skin is a 'complicated network', the writer suggests that you can prevent illness with a hot bath <u>as it</u> opens the pores of your skin.

**b** For example:

- The writer advises that you should never take a bath immediately after eating because it could be dangerous, <u>although</u> you can if you 'allow three hours to elapse'.

- <u>Because</u> it could be dangerous, the writer advises that you should never take a bath immediately after eating, <u>although</u> you can if you 'allow three hours to elapse'.

**2** For example: The writer suggests that people who don't bathe are like pigs when she explains that baths help you digest food properly and that clean pigs produce better-quality meat.

For example: The writer explains that baths help you digest food properly because clean pigs produce better-quality meat and this suggests that people who don't bathe are like pigs.

## Page 70

For example:

The writer gives the reader some ~~pretty serious~~ <u>very forceful</u> ~~warnings~~ <u>advice</u> about when to have a bath. She says, 'Never take a bath, or in any way immerse yourself in water, immediately after having eaten; a bath would be distinctly dangerous'. The words 'never' and 'in any way' ~~make it sound like~~ <u>imply</u> this is ~~really important~~ <u>vital</u> and the word 'dangerous' ~~sounds like~~ <u>suggests</u> ~~she's~~ <u>she is</u> trying to ~~scare~~ <u>alarm</u> the reader. <u>Although</u> she ~~doesn't say~~ <u>does not explain</u> why it is dangerous, ~~you get the idea~~ <u>it creates the impression</u> that you really must ~~do what she says~~ <u>follow her advice</u>.

Published by Pearson Education Limited, 80 Strand, London, WC2R 0RL.

www.pearsonschoolsandfecolleges.co.uk

Text © Pearson Education Limited 2017
Produced and typeset by Tech-Set Ltd, Gateshead

The right of David Grant to be identified as author of this work has been asserted by him in accordance with the Copyright, Designs and Patents Act 1988.

First published 2017

20 19 18 17
10 9 8 7 6 5 4 3 2 1

**British Library Cataloguing in Publication Data**
A catalogue record for this book is available from the British Library

ISBN 978 0435 18318 9

Printed in Slovakia by Neografia

*We are grateful to the following for permission to reproduce copyright material:*

**Source A** on page 2 from *The Midwich Cuckoos* Penguin (John Wyndham 2008) pp.14–15, The Midwich Cuckoos by John Wyndham (Penguin, 2008). Reproduced with permission of David Higham Associates Ltd ; **Source A** on page 18 from *The Life of Ian Fleming*, 1st ed., Bloomsbury Ac (John Pearson 2013) pp. 266–268, Extract from The Life of Ian Fleming by John Pearson reprinted by permission of Peters Fraser & Dunlop (www.petersfraserdunlop.com) on behalf of John Pearson; **Source A** on page 26 from Experience: I fell out of the sky, *Guardian* 09/05/2014 (Matthew Blake; Neil Laughton), https://www.theguardian.com/lifeandstyle/2014/may/09/experience-i-fell-out-of-the-sky, Copyright Guardian News & Media Ltd 2016; **Source A** on page 34 from *The Unlikely Pilgrimage Of Harold Fry*, Black Swan (Rachel Joyce 2013) pp.11–13, Excerpt(s) from THE UNLIKELY PILGRIMAGE OF HAROLD FRY: A NOVEL by Rachel Joyce, copyright © 2012 by Rachel Joyce. Used by permission of Random House, an imprint and division of Penguin Random House LLC. All rights reserved. and Rachel Joyce, *The Unlikely Pilgrimage Of Harold Fry*, copyright © Rachel Joyce 2013, reprinted by permission of Conville & Walsh Ltd on behalf of Rachel Joyce; **Source A** on page 42 from *'Poison' Someone Like You*, Penguin Modern Classics (Roald Dahl 2009) pp.117–118, Reprinted with permission of David Higham Associates Limited.; **Source B** on page 50 from *The Life And Times Of The Thunderbolt Kid: Travels Through my Childhood*, Black Swan (Bill Bryson) pp. 262–263, Excerpt(s) from THE LIFE AND TIMES OF THE THUNDERBOLT KID: A MEMOIR by Bill Bryson, copyright © 2006 by Bill Bryson. Used by permission of Broadway Books, an imprint of the Crown Publishing Group, a division of Penguin Random House LLC. All rights reserved. and Reprinted with permission of Bill Bryson; **Source A** on page 58 from *Never Cry Wolf: Amazing True Story of Life Among Arctic Wolves* 1st Back Bay Pbk., Little Brown (Farley Mowat) 161,; **Source 3** on page 75 from *Going Commando* John Blake Publishing Ltd (Mark Time 2015), From Going Commando by Mark Time, Published by John Blake Publishing